Presenter Evolution

Featuring the revolutionary presentation planning tool

The "Cadence Charting System"

First Edition | 2019

ISBN 978-0-578-55750-2

Web: www.mikebrian.com

LinkedIn: Mike Brian

Facebook: @mikebrianspeaks

To book Mike to speak at your event or for bulk purchase discounts,
please visit www.mikebrian.com

Who to thank for their help in bringing this book to life?

I guess first and foremost, I am thankful to my Father in Heaven for the opportunities, talents and abilities I have been given to develop in my life. Also, my parents and especially my dear mother for dealing with all of the other parents complaining that my stories were freaking their kids out.

To my amazing kids: Maddie, Collin, Alayna and Ryker for standing beside me throughout my career and supporting me in my crazy entrepreneurial journeys.

To my awesome company Penna Powers for providing the opportunities and canvas for my career. This is a company of incredibly intelligent and creative people that I have, and always will, consider my family.

Most importantly, thank you to my sweetheart and true inspiration of my life. She is the woman that would sacrifice everything for my happiness. The woman that lovingly pushes me to be a better person and trusts that I can do whatever I set my mind to—Annie.

Introduction

Every one of us is a presenter, whether we like it or not. You may not believe this notion, but just think about it; when you pull up to a drive-through window, you "present" what you would like to order to the person hiding behind the backlit sign. When you argue with someone or even just state your opinion, you are actually "presenting" your thoughts and ideas. Even the most timid people do this type of presentation every day. I like to think about the first presentation on earth, which took place a long time ago to a couple who lived in a really beautiful garden. Life was good, and everything was working out perfectly for them, until one day, a salesman unexpectedly came along that persuaded them to trade everything they had for an opportunity that they really didn't completely understand. Yes, this is the age-old story of Adam and Eve in the Garden of Eden as found in the Bible. I believe they experienced the first sales presentation, and if you think about it, Lucifer did a great job. He presented the benefits and made his offering very enticing. He experienced rejection and turned to an influencer to help him persuade them. He was eventually able to overcome any opposition from them, and both Adam and Eve, maybe not really knowing all the ramifications of that decision, bought the deal.

That first presentation got us to where the human family is today. We are all giving or receiving presentations, in one form or another, all of the time. Hopefully, we don't have the same sinister motives as that first presenter.

I think it's fascinating when you put most people on a stage or in front of a group, they become like a deer in the headlights: locked up, unable to think, and wondering why they are instantly sweating from every pore. Others would rather be "burned in a fire" as Jerry Seinfeld once said in a monologue. For some, however, presenting in front of a group of people isn't an unpleasant experience. They are very comfortable with it and seem to enjoy the spotlight.

This book is for those who are, or long to be, comfortable presenting in front of an audience but want to get better. It's for those who know audience engagement is important but are not quite sure how to make it happen. It's for those who know better than to read straight from PowerPoint slides but still don't know what content to display. This book may be just the ticket to open your mind to a new way of thinking about your presentations. It will help you think about what the audience is experiencing versus what you are trying to say.

Professionals who present on a regular basis become very good at watching their audience. Their comfort level and fear are completely under control, and they are focused on what they want the audience to get out of their presentation. As a marketing and advertising professional, I have dedicated over three decades to creating and perfecting a "Cadence Charting Technique" to be used in planning and developing a presentation. One of the purposes of this book is to show you how to use this technique and empower you with the ability to implement it. You will learn to look at your presentation in a whole new light and develop it, not just by organizing your thoughts, but by strategically structuring your information in a way that will captivate, and more importantly, communicate with your audience.

"Presentation skills are worthy of extremely obsessive study."
- Tom Peters

Chapter 1
The Evolution of Presenting

We've been presenting since we could communicate, and for the most part, we're pretty good at it in a one-on-one situation. However, when we think of getting in front of a group, many of us seem to feel that we are being critically judged. It makes us feel like we've forgotten an article of clothing—or worse! Our hearts start to pound, and before we know it, we're seeing stars and dripping bullets of sweat.

Some people feel that they will never get the hang of it. They have a false belief that you're either a good presenter or you're not. If you are reading this book, you're not one of the people that believe you're as good as you'll ever get. You're looking for ways to improve and become more comfortable and confident while presenting. I intend to give you the knowledge and tools necessary to help you look at your presentations from a new paradigm and become an engaging and successful presenter.

Two of the many objectives for giving a presentation are first to convince or persuade others of something, and second to communicate a complex message. Years ago people used to create prototypes or drawings of their ideas and lay them out during their presentations. Back then, you had to be a very good physical presenter to be successful because you didn't have dozens of visuals to lean on. It was up to you and your voice to captivate, educate, and motivate the room.

Today there are dozens of software tools and technical systems that can, if used properly, really help a presenter achieve their goals and reach their audience.

The Old Days

In the old information-dumping kind of presentations, presenters would compile a deck of acetate slides or a pile of handouts full of the information they were going to present and simply act as the voice delivering it, one slide or sheet at a time. These presentations were focused on getting all of the information out into the open. Often, the audience was required to be there and some kind of bribe usually accompanied the "invitation" to attend. Inevitably, somewhere in the room, a person had folded a piece of paper into a triangle football and someone else held up their fingers as goalpost. Not a great sign.

I once attended a presentation by Stephen R. Covey who wrote The Seven Habits of Highly Effective People. As the presentation was about to begin, his Sherpa *(or his presentation engineer—whatever you'd like to call him)* came into the room and was walking toward the overhead projector with a 4-inch binder of acetates. With about five feet to go, he tripped on the power cable! The binder hit the ground and the slides slid about 10 feet across the floor. With a look of panic on his face, he turned to a small group of attendees that had arrived early and yelled, "Nobody touch anything!" He methodically picked up the slides and thumbed through them quickly to make sure they were in the right order. Mr. Covey came in and gave the presentation without knowing what had happened. The presentation engineer was amazingly calm and checked each slide before Mr. Covey presented it. Fortunately, everything worked out perfectly.

Modern technology has, thankfully, eliminated the need for this kind of assistance and the accompanying potential for a misstep.

Winging It

Have you ever been in a presentation where the presenter was just winging it? Admittedly, there are a handful of people who can actually do this. However, in order for them to do it well, they must have a vast understanding of the topic and some natural ability, along with a command of their industry language. Most people, even the very educated and experienced speakers, find it difficult to hold a train of thought and move through information without at least a simple structure.

Often, those who are put on the spot or attempt to wing a presentation fall victim to a battery of challenges. Take body ticks, for example. These presenters might use hand gestures erratically or unconsciously shrug their shoulders. They might engage vocal ticks like 'uh' or 'um,' or worse, 'like,' as crutches or space-takers between thoughts. Some people resort to just stringing together a bunch of non-related stories that help them chew through their allotted time.

When these things happen, these presenters find it very difficult to keep their audience engaged.

Today's Tool Kit

We've come a long way in techniques and technology in the presentation arena. The days of paper presentations, chalk board talks, overhead acetates, or 35mm slides have been replaced with slick software and projection systems that empower presenters like never before. This is both a good thing and a bad thing.

As our presentation skills and abilities progressed over the years, we went from mimeographed handouts *(remember the purple inked papers?)* to photocopies, then from photocopies to acetates on an overhead projector *(remember the wax pencils used to write on them?)* Eventually, companies came out with revolutionary software to produce 35mm slides. Aldus Persuasion was one of the first software packages that produced them. The software had a Preview mode that showed on your computer screen what the slide would look like when it was printed. At that time, there wasn't a laptop available that had video out capabilities, so in order to display the slides, you had to either use a 35mm slide printer and pack in your projector or print them out on acetate slides and use an overhead projector. Either way, this was a vast improvement over writing on a chalk board or scribbling on a blank acetate.

In 1989, I was the marketing director for a travel agency in Salt Lake City. While there, I developed the capability to produce newspaper and magazine ads in-house, along with a number of other communication tools for our clients. One day, the president of the company called me into his office and said that we had a problem in our corporate sales division. He told me that our major competitor was beating us three out of five times in our presentations. He asked me to figure out how this was happening and to find a solution. After a few months of research, I realized that they weren't doing anything unique in their presentations. They had simply convinced their audience that they were more capable than we were because they owned a chartered airline. The frustrating thing about that was they didn't actually own the airline! The travel agency and the charter airline company just used the same name. We were dealing with a perception, not a fact.

Realizing that it wasn't necessarily a product or service issue but a perception issue, I went to work trying to figure out how to fix this problem. Our agency even opened our own charter airline to compete. As it turns out, trying to be a travel agency and an airline creates a level of competition with actual airlines. They didn't really appreciate that, so we shut it down. During that time, I heard about a research project that was being discussed on a radio show *(the Internet hadn't been invented yet)* that said something to the effect that in situations where political and relational values were equal, the presentation would win the deal up to 80% of the time.

This was an aha! moment for me. I felt that this might be the way to overcome the issue of perception, so I went to work on our presentation. I created a system that used a huge television projector, about the size of a tuba, and a patch cable that would turn the signal from a Macintosh CX computer into a RCA signal for the projector. The only problem was the scan rate of the computer didn't match the projector so there was an annoying line crawling down the screen over and over again. But that didn't seem to matter because it was so much more innovative than an overhead projector or 35mm slides. In fact, the whizzbang of the system often blew the prospect's mind. It pushed us into a whole new perception window. And we started winning more business with it.

In October 1991, Apple computer released the MacBook 170. It was a black and white laptop with no video out capabilities. That year, I worked with a company in Oregon that developed a digital video converter card. This card could be soldered onto the motherboard of the Mac 170 and generate a solid RGB signal out. Soon after, Proxima released a digital LCD screen that could lie on top of an overhead projector and project the computer screen. BOOM! This was a game changer. Not only could I carry all of the equipment in by myself but the visuals looked professional and solid.

In 1992, I was presenting to KSL Television, the NBC affiliate in Salt Lake City, to manage a trip for their major clients. We had never won any of these trips because of a political relationship KSL had with another agency that we just couldn't overcome. So, I decided that I had nothing to lose. I pulled out all the stops and went in hard with my new fancy presentation system. During the presentation, the station's general sales manager stopped me. Right in the middle of the presentation he said, "Okay, who did this?" I responded with, "Did what?" He asked, "Who put this presentation and this system together for you?" I said, "Um, I did." He then took me out into the hallway and said, "Okay, I'll get you this trip if you'll come in here and show us how to do what you're doing in there."

It worked. I had actually overcome a political relationship with sizzle! We won that bid, and three months later I started my interactive marketing company, ProClix, with the NBC affiliate as my first client.

That began my career as a presentation consultant. I used all of my marketing and advertising training, along with a bit of my theater background, and began cultivating experience in the trade. Over the span of 30 years, I've been able to explore the presentation world from soup to nuts. I merged ProClix Interactive with PPCH, a Salt Lake City based, full-service advertising agency, following a partnership project with the 2002 Winter Olympics. Our agency is now called Penna Powers, and we have evolved far beyond a traditional agency into a professional communications firm that manages all forms of communications, from advertising to public relations, and from digital production to social change. We work with companies on their internal communications and train their leadership on presentation development and delivery, as well as other leadership skills.

With the invention of presentation software, we entered into a new era of presentations. And WOW, they were horrible for a while! They went from being designed to produce 35mm slides to full-screen multimedia presentations. I used to have a business card that said: "Just because you can, doesn't mean you should." This common English phrase really summed up the use of presentation software for me. Every time the software manufacturers would add a feature, you would see it overused or grossly misused. For example, the slide transition. Yes, you can now make the transitions between your slides do several dazzling effects. But for crying out loud, ask yourself the question, "Should I use them all in a single presentation just because I can?"

People also overuse other features of presentation software. Instead of using a planning technique, they just start slamming content onto their slides and shuffle them around until they feel good about it. I'm not sure anything could be worse. This capability is dangerous and makes it easy to just add something whenever and wherever you want, just because you can.

I was at a presentation where a professional motivational speaker was delivering his message. I kept saying to myself, "Okay, he isn't bad." But then the unthinkable happened.

Suddenly there was an erroneous photograph of himself in a pickup truck with a young girl on the screen. There were over 300 people in the room, and he was on a strong upward roll with his content. BOOM! He came to a screeching halt. He tuned to the screen and said, "Oh, sorry, I was working on my presentation on the flight out here and must have put this shot of me with my daughter in by accident. Well, while I have this up here let me tell you about her." The room was in shock. I was having the time of my life watching him try to get the fragmented story out and tie it into his message. When he finally realized that there was no bridge for him to cross the topic, he just said, "Well, that's my daughter, and we're in our truck." You could almost hear crickets. I thought to myself, "That just happened?" It took him three more screens to get the audience back and wrap up. Later, I spoke to the event planner who hired him and asked how much it cost to have him come. The answer was, "too much."

Presentation software is an amazing tool in the hands of a true presentation developer. But when I sit at the back of an airplane and watch dozens of people "hacking" away at presentations, it makes me cringe. I have heard the expression, "Death by PowerPoint" many times. The comment is not directed at PowerPoint; the Microsoft software is amazing, and in the right hands it is a professional weapon. But in the wrong hands . . . well, let's just say it's not pretty.

Another element that has changed the landscape of presenting is access to assets. Assets being photos, graphics, videos, and other content. Again, you would think that these would only make presenting easier and better, but exercise caution. I love The Far Side comic strip books, but I am pretty sure that Gary Larson never intended for The Far Side images to end up in professional presentations. However, I see them everywhere. Mr. Larson is a comic genius, but do they belong in a professional presentation? Sometimes having one that fits the situation perfectly is fun, but overused, they can really upset your rhythm. Also, the use of pirated or hacked visuals is out of control. You want a slide in your presentation that shows that the top 10 companies on the planet are your clients? It takes about three minutes to pull their logos from the internet. That is a dangerous ability. Not only is it dangerous from a legal perspective, but it is tempting for people to just keep adding and adding visuals to their presentation. This bloating effect makes it very hard to stay on topic and on time.

It's tempting to surf Google until they find a floating image that fits the bill. They'll either snag a screen shot or download it thinking that they aren't planning on making money on their presentation so they don't really need to buy it. Well, that isn't how it works. Using someone's work without permission is not okay, even if you don't think that the presentation will ever be seen again. At the next presentation you attend, notice how many people are whipping out their phones and snapping photos of the slides. Besides being unethical, it will take only one person to fire that photo off in their Instagram or Facebook account and it's out. The repercussions can be brutal. Always ask for permission to use images or purchase them for your use.

When a presenter is using technology, they can easily turn the control of the presentation over to the technology, meaning that the presentation takes over. The person running the slides could just be at the back of the room and advance the slides until the deck is complete. The mistake of over-producing a presentation is common with people who are nervous or worried about getting their message across. People can only manage so much stimuli during a presentation. If your screen has 10 bullet points on it, and you're just going to read them off, I guarantee that the audience will disconnect from both channels of communication.

At the end of the day, getting better at presenting is simply an equation of knowing what to do and then practicing it. Hopefully you're reading this book to learn a few things that will help you do just that. We have amazing tools at our disposal today, and the key to utilizing those tools and making them work great is knowing how to use them effectively.

Should You Be Presenting?

Having coached many presenters over the years, one of the most difficult positions I often get placed in is the awkward role of telling an executive that they aren't the best fit to present in certain situations. These people are the Presidents, CEOs, senior leaders, and oftentimes the inventor or entrepreneur who started the business. If you think about it, in many other positions within an organization, people may not have the opportunity to formally present, so there isn't a need to tell them that they shouldn't. The executives, however, are expected to be able to present. It comes with the job, so to speak.

Chapter 1 ~ The Evolution of Presenting

Years ago, our agency was hired to help a firm with their leadership's presentation skills as well as develop a presentation for their sales efforts. They had us conduct a presenter's workshop that gave 15 of their senior staff an opportunity to go through our training and develop a presentation. Each person would have five minutes to present their 10-slide presentation, and then we would critique them—in private, obviously. The objective of this workshop was two-fold: first, to provide their leadership with professional development training; and second, to identify which members of their team should do the sales presenting for the firm.

While the people were working on their presentations, I received a call from one of the company's senior staff members. They wanted to go to lunch to discuss something. I was concerned at first because I was afraid that I might have offended someone at their company, and they were going to fire us. But that wasn't it. Three of their staff came to the lunch and said to me, "This is going great, but we really need you to tell the eight partners that are in the group that they can't present the company to prospective clients anymore. They are killing us every time we get the opportunity to pitch business." After a minute of processing

mikebrian.com   25 what they were telling me, I said, "Okay, let me see if I understand you correctly. You want me to tell the partners and owners of your company that they are horrible presenters and that they shouldn't present. Is that correct?" They all answered "Yes!" in unison, and then one of them said, "None of us dare to tell them because we work for them all day, and we love them and don't want to hurt their feelings."

 As you can imagine, these situations put me in an incredibly uncomfortable position. Yet, as I evaluated their presentations, they were right. Not that the partners were horrible, but several people in the company were much better presenters. The night after the presentations, I lay in bed thinking, "How am I going to tell these partners, the folks who are going to pay our bill, that they shouldn't present?" Then it hit me. After years of pushing through this type of painful task, I realized something. It wasn't so much that they were terrible presenters, it was just that they couldn't present at the level their audience perceived them. They were partners of the company, and their prospects perceived them as company royalty and industry leaders. When they walk in the room and introduce themselves, they are at their highest perceived value, a partner of the firm. If they take a role beyond introducing their team, they become employees of the firm, just regular people who work at the company. And if they are not killer presenters, their equity erodes. This isn't me spinning the message into a swallowable pill. This is a simple fact. If you can't present at the level of your perceived value, you should use someone else, someone who is a great presenter and can represent the company well.

For the first time, without flogging their egos, I helped these executives realize that they could be more impactful introducing their presentation team and then moderating the question and answer period at the end of the presentation. Needless to say, the company found great success with this new understanding. These executives now handle internal and existing client presentations where their equity supports them because they have a deep, endearing relationship with the audience.

My motivation for writing this book emerged from a dawning realization that many very successful businesspeople are missing some basic, but powerful, presentation skills. In fact, in 2009 at Columbia University, Warren Buffett said, "Right now, I would pay $100,000 for ten percent of the future earnings of any of you, so if you're interested, see me after class."

After the laughter subsided, he turned serious and said, "Now, you can improve your value by 50 percent just by learning communication skills—public speaking. If that's the case, see me after class, and I'll pay you $150,000."

I couldn't agree with him more. I believe that by becoming a proficient communicator and speaker, you will increase your value up to 50%. With that conviction, I have consolidated 35 years of experience in the communication and presentation field into what I believe are five key areas that great presenters in the world have mastered. And I believe that anyone can become a better presenter by working on and developing these skills and techniques.

Action is a great restorer and builder of confidence. Inaction is not only the result, but the cause of fear. Perhaps the action you take will be successful; perhaps different action or adjustments will have to follow. But any action is better than no action at all.

–Norman Vincent Peale

Chapter 2
Confidence

Where Does Fear Come From?

Fear seems to be the most crippling emotion for a presenter. Where does fear come from? I believe that fear was intrinsically built into humans as a survival instinct. Think about the moments you experience fear and what that emotion does to you. Your heart rate increases, your adrenaline pumps, and your senses are shot into hyper mode. It is the moment of fight or flight. You may not be getting chased by a lion, but presenting is considered by many as one the most frightening things in the world. Comedians talk about it because it seems weird to them. I heard one say that most people would rather be the one in the coffin than the one speaking at the funeral. I argue that if you can learn to channel the emotions that attack at the moment you stand up to speak and turn them into a controlled level of energy, you'll be surprised by how much power they can give you. Controlling your emotions is critical, and practicing it is the only way you'll learn how. The objective isn't to remove the anxiety before you present but to turn it into a power that can help you.

Working with one of the most successful bankers in the United States, I experienced someone who could elegantly manage any negotiation meeting. Building a very successful career as a professional business banker, he was promoted into a leadership position and was tasked with making a presentation at a client conference. At that meeting, there would be over 400 clients in attendance. Our agency was hired to develop their presentations, and I spent a few hours with each presenter working with them on their delivery.

I was shocked to see this executive pacing around the stage with sweat running down his face and incoherent words coming out of his mouth. We sat down and worked through his content, and I asked him why he was so wound up. He said that he hated presenting more than anything on earth, but he knew it came with the job. That blew my mind. I decided to break down the situation with him to see if I could settle him down a bit. First issue: I assured him that no one in that room knew more about his topic than he did. Nobody was going to call him out or "boo" him from the audience. Second issue: Every one of the clients respected him as a professional. In fact, they loved him. He was approachable and fun, and they couldn't wait to hear from him. Third issue: Everyone presenting at the conference was nervous. It's a natural reaction. All he needed to do was remember that this was a room full of his friends and no matter how his presentation went, they would still love him.

I worked in a soft, humorous opening that gave him a minute or two to connect with the audience before he went into his topic. From the control booth, I was praying hard that he would get the reaction from the audience that he needed to calm down. His first sentence made me want to crawl into a hole and disappear, but then he cleared his throat and delivered his opening. From that moment on, he nailed the presentation, and everyone loved it.

I always tell people that they really have nothing to worry about because no one in the room is going to jump out of their seat and attack them. However, one day I had a funny experience that challenged that notion. I was conducting a presenter's workshop to a group of public safety officers, and when I made that comment, I had a shocking and hilarious realization—everyone in that room had a weapon. When I shared that thought with them, I got a roar of laughter and then the audience went right back to being police officers. I didn't get a single positive body language cue during the entire workshop (*I think they're trained to do that*). But I came out unscathed, even though it was one of the most tense presentations of my career.

Being nervous to present is normal. Great presenters have learned how to turn that emotion into fuel. They actually get a high out of it. They channel it into their opening and use it to launch their presentation strong. This is the moment that you set the expectation of your presentation.

Tactics:

- Take some time and write down your fears about presenting. Once you have them documented, you can address them individually.

- Create a routine to do before you present that will calm you down and get you in the right frame of mind.

- Steer away from energy drinks or caffeine gum—they'll just give you the jitters.

- Don't let fear stop you from presenting; channel your energy and practice.

Overcoming Personal Obstacles

As I mentioned earlier, the increase in adrenalin and blood flowing through your body can make you react differently than you normally would. Body and verbal tics and/or other crutches are anomalies that occur when this happens. They are typically things that people don't do in normal situations or when they are just having a casual conversation. When put in the spotlight, their arms, legs, and mouth just start to freak out.

Physical body tics can be very distracting. Here is a list of some of the issues I've experienced with my clients over the years:

Pacing: Walking back and forth across the stage for no rhyme or reason.

Kung Fu Grip: Speaking at a podium and hanging on to it like your life depends on it.

Limb Malfunction: Arms, hands, and feet simply have no motor control. They end up just hanging out in space or locking into an awkward position.

Remote Phobia: The presentation remote becomes the center of your universe. You feel like it's the most fragile object in the world yet you're gripping it like your lifeline.

The Three Step: This is hard to see in real-time, but the presenter uses one foot as a pivot and the other foot to step forward and backward creating the illusion that the presenter is moving when really, they aren't.

Shaky Hands Syndrome: You try to make a gesture and as your hands come out, they start shaking like a leaf.

mikebrian.com

Blindness: The thought of making eye contact with someone in the audience is out of the question because you're afraid someone might give you the "What are you saying?" look.

Nothing happens: I mean nothing. You don't move, speak, or even breathe. The next thing you know, you're waking up off stage with someone waving smelling salts under your nose.

Overcoming physical body tics requires that you are put in an uncomfortable situation frequently but before you can overcome them, you have to know what they are. The best way to identify them is to have someone videotape you giving a presentation. After you have settled down, watch it. I know, no one likes how they look or sound on video, but just take notes on your movements, speech flow, and eye contact. Are you moving with a purpose or just wandering around? Are you talking like an auctioneer? Do you notice there is an audience, and are you connecting with them? Notice your arm movements, your gestures, and your physical placement in the room. If you're speaking from a podium, are you gripping it like it's a flotation device? Are you holding so still that you have become part of the podium? Then, pick a couple that seem the most distracting and make a plan to overcome them. Remember, people get better at what they practice. If you dedicate the time to overcoming your distracting habits, you'll not only present better, but you'll be more comfortable doing it. Don't just list the bad things you see, note the good things you do as well and continue refining them.

Tactics:

- Videotape and critique yourself.

- Practice in front of others and ask them to look for crutches you might be using.

- Start noticing tics that you see in other presenters— evaluate yourself to see if you are experiencing the same tics.

- Don't let your tics stop you from presenting. Acknowledging them and practicing are the only way to break the habit.

The Pre-game Show

One of the secret tactics of great speakers is their pre-game routine. Some people's routines don't happen until right before they speak. Others start the day before. Mine is very simple. I am careful NOT to eat too much within two hours of speaking. I stay away from caffeine and soda the day of my presentation, and finally, right before I speak, I do a quick self-talk. I reassure myself that I am confident, prepared, and no one is going to attack me on the stage. That thought makes me chuckle a little, and it seems to calm me down.

Some speakers have a detailed regimen or routine to get them through their presentation. A few examples:

1. Exercise for 30 minutes the morning of a presentation.

2. Eat pasta for dinner the night before to get your energy up for the morning.

3. Drink a sugar-free Red Bull mixed with a Diet Pepsi two hours before. *(This is dangerous, but it works for them.)*

4. Wear a lucky tie or scarf.

5. Keep a sentimental or lucky item in a pocket.

6. Gargle with warm water and lemon juice.

You may think these are silly, but they are some of the actual tactics I have experienced and witnessed over the years. The important thing to remember is that you shouldn't be worked up. You will perform your very best if you are at your natural state of being. Do everything you can to keep things as constant and normal as possible. Don't worry, there will be plenty of adrenaline to get you going. Don't add unnecessary elements that may throw you off.

Having too many elements in your pre-game routine is also dangerous. If you have a 24-hour routine to get ready to present, you may periodically experience an unplanned interruption that could throw the whole plan out of whack. Mentally, you put yourself at risk in these situations. If missing an element of your routine paralyzes you, you need to simplify it.

Learning to be calm is probably the most important thing to master. Going into a presentation with your heart pounding and your head swimming is going to cause your body to freak out and your thoughts to fragment. Practice a few things that calm you down and build them into your routine. I have an associate who is a salesperson for a financial institution. We were at lunch one day, and he confided in me that he hates the presenting part of sales more than anything, but he makes good money so he has had to figure out how to love it. His tactic was very interesting. The morning of his presentation he gets a McMuffin, a hash brown, and an OJ. Then, on his way to the presentation he plays his favorite music in his car as loud as he can. He told me that somehow the music calms him down and he stops worrying about what he has to do. After the presentation, he grabs a Coke Zero as a reward and jams to his music again all the way back to the office. A simple routine that seems to work for him has helped him to enjoy what he considers the most stressful part of his job. He has learned to use a simple routine as a tool. If you practice presenting, you're going to get better at it. You'll be asked to present more and . . . you see where this is going. Practice creates progress. Reward yourself with something like a movie, or a round of golf or a massage if that helps you prepare and execute your presentation goals.

A word of caution here. My father-in-law gave me some sound advice early in my career. He warned me to never reward my successes with food. He said, "You're good at what you do, and I'm afraid that if you always reward yourself with a treat, you'll be morbidly obese before you know it." Your presentation pre-game and post-game routines need to be simple and designed around things that make you feel good and normal.

Tactics:

- Create a pre-game routine that has elements you can control.

- Practice creates progress—you perfect what you practice.

- Use rewards to motivate you—use caution when it comes to food, as you get better, you might start gaining weight.

- Adrenaline is the only stimulant you need. Steer clear from any additional stimulants.

- Your routine is a very personal tool, so do what makes you feel normal and calm.

Research Your Venue

Some of the venues or conference rooms that you present in will be better than others. It is a great idea to scope out the room prior to your presentation. Sometimes this isn't possible, but most of the time, even if it's for a sales pitch, you can get in early for a quick look at the technology and the layout of the room. One of the most difficult venues I've had to deal with was while working with the NBC affiliate in Salt Lake City. We were preparing to give a critical presentation to a large media buying group. The venue they selected for the presentation was the President's Club room at the local professional hockey arena. As we walked into the room, I about had a heart attack. The room faced the eastern Wasatch mountains with nearly 50 feet of floor-to-ceiling windows. It was a spectacular view of the snowcapped mountains, but at 10 am it was like presenting in a tanning bed. We did our best to adjust the room, but the presentation visuals were extremely difficult to see.

If you are presenting in a formal setting as a keynote speaker with an AV crew on board, it is also important that you get there early and test their equipment and gear. Nothing will cause you more anxiety than the technology failing right as you walk on stage. It's important that you're prepared with a backup plan just in case something goes wrong.

An optimal venue would be a theater setting where the audience is tiered above you in a half circle, like a university lecture hall. However, most presentations are done in a massive room with unbelievably high ceilings and behemoth chandeliers intended for wedding or gala clients. The audience is either in rows of super thin tables that disappear into the darkness or at round tables where only three people actually have a view. If you are lucky, there are multiple screens showing your presentation, so only a handful of people actually notice you on a raised stage. The fact of the matter is, you usually don't get to pick your venue. So just get over it and learn how to adapt. Getting there early will give you a chance to acclimate and decide how to make the best of whatever situation you are given.

The more you present, the easier it will be to overcome situations where your venue is not on your side. Don't let elements that you can't control impact your mission. You are there to present. Do whatever you have to do to accomplish it. I use humor in most of these situations. Your audience will usually sympathize with you, and this builds your relationship with them as they listen to you present. I would be careful about negative comments slamming the venue. After all, you don't want the power to go out right in the middle of your presentation.

Tactics:

- Call in advance to see if you can site inspect the room where you'll be presenting. If they won't let you, ask for a photo or a least a list of technology that will be available.

- Take a backup projector and a speaker whenever possible.

• Prepare an Emergency Tech Kit *(see Setting Up Your Gear)*, and always have a backup output so you can adapt if technology or the venue fails.

• If the venue is difficult, use gentle humor to expose and acknowledge the issue, and move on.

Get There Early or You're Late

My father-in-law, Wayne Hickenlooper, was a shrewd businessman. He gave me amazing advice throughout my career and taught me early on that "If you are late to your presentation, you will lose equity with the audience exponentially for every minute you're late." In the presentation setting, if you're late and have to rush and get your equipment set up, running around while the audience just watches you, you'll feel their gaze drilling into the back of your head and loose your focus before you even begin.

A few years ago, our agency was pitching a division of the Nevada state government on a big project. Three of our presentation team members flew in the night before for a dress rehearsal with our team from our Las Vegas office. Everything went great in our practice session, and I felt like we were going to nail it. Our presentation was at 9:00 a.m. and we were about 20 minutes from the venue. I suggested that we all meet for breakfast at 7:00 a.m. and then check out and be ready to go by 8:15. That would give us time to settle at their office before we went in to pitch. One of our team members said she would rather sleep for that hour and would meet us in the lobby at 8:15 instead. The next morning, the rest of the team had a nice breakfast, and at 8:15 we were all checked out and ready to go. At 8:25, I texted her and asked if she was okay. No response. At 8:30, I called again and she answered in a full panic. My text woke her up, and she was frantically trying to get dressed, packed, and out the door. At 8:40, we pulled out of the hotel parking lot and raced to the venue. She hadn't showered, and her hair looked like she had ridden a motorcycle to the presentation. We raced into the building where they were waiting for us. Our competitors had completed their presentation and were already gone. We scrambled to get set up and were five minutes late getting started. You can imagine the impact that had on our presentation, especially on her part. She was still in her adrenaline-wake-up state, and the creases on her cheek from the pillow were still visible. Needless to say, no amount of humor can overcome a situation like that. The pressure it put on the presentation team was incredible, and that was the last time she was invited to pitch with my team. Sure, it was an awesome story later, but in the moment, it was unprofessional.

Tactics:

- Program in your head that being late is NOT AN OPTION. Nothing will repair your equity erosion if you're late.

- Buffer your time and take into account anything that may impede your arrival.

- If you are presenting alone, write down a schedule to ensure your prompt arrival. Set multiple alarms in addition to the wake-up call, if necessary.

- If you are traveling, be packed to leave the night before so you can just check out.

Setting Up Your Gear and Backups

I know a lot of presenters who have abandoned the technology gear and just speak because they are afraid of it failing. Well, I believe that presenting is more often a show than a speech. There are a select few people that are simply gifted speakers, and they can move a room at will. However, most of us need the support of visuals to elevate the imagination and retain the attention of the audience. I would argue that even the best speakers would benefit from the right visuals supporting them.

Earlier, I referenced an Emergency Tech Kit. This is a bag that I can toss into my laptop case that has every conceivable connection I might need for a presentation. It gives me great confidence going in to a presentation that I can probably overcome any tech failure. I also won't go to a presentation without my backup projector. I can honestly say that I have only needed it a handful of times, but those few times absolutely compensate for taking it every time.

I was once conducting an offsite presentation workshop with the management team of an international mining company, and I was using their data projector. We were clipping along with the presentation when all of a sudden, their projector bulb blew. Okay, I have had a lot of things go wrong in presentations, but when this bulb blew, it BLEW! It didn't just softly fade out. It snapped and scared me to death. After a few minutes of them laughing their heads off, I got back up on my feet and tried to compose myself. Three of them grabbed their cell phones and started trying to line up another projector. I calmly said, "I have my backup projector, let's just use it so we can keep going." They all just stared at me for a minute. Right then and there, I realized that this was a moment that I needed to adapt my training and talk about having a backup plan. It was perfect!

It is so important to have a little time to figure out why your screen isn't showing up on their monitor or figure out why your sound isn't going through their system. In fact, most of the time when you hook up to a new system, the monitor settings will default to a factory mode. You'll need a bit of time to adjust your computer to get it working smoothly. As technology progresses, it's getting much easier. In the past, setting up a laptop to a foreign projection system was a crap shoot with horrible odds against you. Thankfully, now, in many situations, you'll be hooking into a huge LCD television monitor via an HDMI cable. These connections vary from manufacturer to manufacturer. Keep a proven HDMI cable in your case in the event their cable fails.

When it comes to backups, there are a lot of options. I use Apple's Keynote software to present. I always adapt the presentation and have a PowerPoint version of it as well. I also make a PDF version and carry a printed version for the worst-case scenario. I keep a flash drive on my keychain with every possible version of the presentation in case my laptop breaks down or my bag gets swiped. The final line of backup is perhaps the most important: If all else fails, can you give the presentation with no visuals at all? This all goes back to knowing your information and practicing your presentation.

Tactics:

- Prepare an Emergency Tech Kit with cables, dongles, remotes, batteries, and anything else you may need in an emergency.

- Get there early enough to set up and test your equipment.

- Prepare redundancies and carry them in a secure place.

- Always have a backup output so you can adapt if the technology or venue fail.

Let Go of Content and Focus on People

Over the years of coaching executives on presenting, I've noticed how different people use their presentation visuals as a crutch. I am astonished by how many presentations I have seen where every word of the presentation is on the screen. These are moments when people in the audience whisper to each other, "Why didn't they just send us the file? I could have watched this over lunch."

As you practice presenting, you'll find it gets easier to stand up in front of people and talk. As you get more comfortable, you'll find that your presentation will flow much better because it will feel more natural to you. Eventually, you'll reach another level, one that feels like a second wind. At this level, your presentation will be organic, and you will begin to notice and react to your audience more.

Are you making eye contact? Are they paying attention? Is everyone on their phone? Are they falling asleep? Once you begin to see how the audience is responding to your presentation, it will give you opportunities to manage them better. You'll find the people who are paying attention and nodding their heads to your comments. These are your pockets of support. These are the people who are giving you the eye contact you need. If you can learn to gauge how your audience is reacting, it will help you to adjust your cadence to keep your presentation on track.

Tactics:

- Know your information and practice the presentation until it feels natural.

- Take a few seconds at the beginning of your presentation and isolate a few people you will try to connect with.

- Adjust your cadence to keep the momentum of your presentation on track. If you feel you are losing the audience, break your cadence or rhythm with a story or ask a question to get them re-engaged.

Eye Contact and Body Language Signals

At one particular conference, I was presenting to a group of traffic engineers on the art of presenting. I love engineers and realize their brains work very differently than my own. Every time I work with a group of scientists or engineers, I have learned to work on one very specific element of their presentations. I make them memorize this line in regard to visuals in their presentations: "If you have to say, 'I know you can't read this but…' leave it out." I think that due to the scientific nature of their jobs they feel that without the entire spreadsheet on the screen, the information is incomplete. Often their presentations end up being work meetings going over several screens of spreadsheets, which is fine if that's the objective. But if they are presenting to a group of non-engineers, it's problematic at best.

One of my goals at this conference was to teach them about engaging the audience. As I started the presentation, I asked a few questions. They were questions that engineers would know the answers to and they were awesome at answering. In fact, I had to choke them off to keep the presentation cadence on track. While I was conducting the initial Q&A, I was taking note of the people who were going to be my reactors in the audience.

It's difficult to make eye contact with an entire audience if the group is very large. In that case, you need to select a few people to be your reactor anchors. I break the room into four quarters and identify two or three people in each quarter that I can make eye contact with. That eye contact isn't just to have them look at you, it's your mechanism to see if you are communicating with them. In fact, I like to refer to it as face contact. Their eyes are the hook, but it's the expression on their face that gives you the indicator if you're reaching them or not.

If eye contact is uncomfortable or distracting to you, move your anchors out deeper into the audience. Instead of identifying an anchor in the first three rows, go back to the tenth row and pick a few people. Please don't stare at these people. The eye contact is just helping you stay connected to the audience and providing you with facial expressions that help you gauge if they are with you or not.

I have learned over the years that some expressions mean different things. You'll have to make a determination if the expression is the one you are working toward or not. For example, if I am presenting, and I see a few of my anchors with their eyebrows furrowed and their hand rubbing their chin, that could mean, "Hmm, that is a very interesting thought," or it could mean, "I have no idea what he is talking about." They look very similar. To determine which expression you're dealing with, go to a few other anchors and see if any of them are leaning toward one or the other. If any of them are shaking their heads or looking around to see if anyone else is lost, you probably have your answer. If you still can't read the indicator, stop and ask if anyone has any questions about what you just presented.

Eye contact, or should I say face contact, is a powerful tool that will provide you with the feedback you need to gauge if your presentation is working.

Tactics:

- Break the room into quarters and identify a few reactor anchors in each group.

- Don't just focus on the first row of people.

- Eye contact is the hook, but notice facial expressions: face contact.

- If you can't determine what the facial expression is, look at a few others for confirmation. If more than a few look confused, stop and ask if there are any questions.

Confidence is critical in becoming a comfortable and impactful presenter. It builds as you increase your knowledge of the topic, formulate your content and thoughts, and above all, practice. Just keep the thought I mentioned earlier in mind: *You perfect what you practice.* You still may not become a professional speaker after giving the same presentation hundreds of times, but that isn't the point. Gaining confidence as a presenter is more than just perfecting your content. It's about becoming comfortable on the stage or at the mic. Crossing all of the T's and dotting all of the I's in the physical aspects of your presentation will help you focus on the emotional side. Working toward rising above your presentation and focusing on how you are managing the audience is the tipping point of effective presenting.

Passion is energy. Feel the power that comes from focusing on what excites you.

- Oprah Winfrey

Chapter 3
Passion

What is passion? Merriam-Webster defines it in our context as "Intense, driving or an overmastering feeling or conviction," or "A strong liking or desire for or devotion to some activity, object, or concept." I feel that passion is also a conviction to a principle or belief that defines us. Presenting with passion simply means that you are committed to the message you are presenting. It is very difficult to present a topic that you aren't passionate about. You can do it, but the lack of passion typically shows through. Presenting with passion doesn't mean that you cry during your presentation; it means that you demonstrate you are committed to your message. Passion is usually conveyed through your tone and your body language. Presenters also need to be aware that sometimes their passion, or the over-expression of that passion, can backfire on them. Not everyone has the same level of passion on specific topics; in fact, some may actually be equally passionate about the opposite.

Controlled passion helps a presenter stay motivated, provides them with fuel to navigate the cadence of their presentation, and generates the emotion and target objective of their presentation.

Making the Message *Your* Message

When you are presenting to your staff, a client, a prospective client or an interest group, you may engage information about your topic that comes from a variety of sources. It is important and ethical to mention those sources, but it is also critical that you communicate what compelled you to include it. By doing so, you demonstrate ownership of the message you are delivering.

One of the greatest books of our day is How to Win Friends and Influence People by Dale Carnegie. In this book, Mr. Carnegie demonstrates, through dozens of ideas and stories, how you can relate to others and get what you want out of them. Ironically, nothing in his book is new. Everything he writes about is common sense and seemingly obvious. Yet, when I read his book, I found myself saying, "Yeah, I need to be better at that." By so doing, I take ownership of that trait or tactic. Many of the principles in Mr. Carnegie's book resonate strongly with me, and I try to implement them in my life. In fact, at my wife's suggestion, I read the book every year in an attempt to keep its principles at the top of my mind. I think it makes me a better human. I guess she thinks so as well.

When I present, some of Mr. Carnegie's topics and strategies surface, not because I am using them to prove or reinforce a point, but because they are part of who I am.

Consume your information and make it part of you. Presenters are much more impactful if the message they are delivering comes from deep inside them. That level of conviction to the topic helps the audience develop stronger emotions simply because the message was delivered in a passionate manner.

We make presentations that convey a message, and as a presenter, our hope is that the audience will consume or receive that message or information in the manner we intended, hopefully with the intent to create change in some way.

Tactics:

- Do your research and use information that you're passionate about. Own the message.

- When using support sources, document the source and connect the information to your message.

- Continue to build on your experiences. What do you believe and why?

- Present as a source, don't just compile others' thoughts and regurgitate them.

Your Appearance and Attitude

One of my heroes is Steve Jobs, not in every aspect of his life, but in a few traits that make him unique to me. In the early years of his career, Jobs would present to the public in a trendy suit or hippie-type colored shirt, which was in keeping with the style at the time. I think he was trying to be what he thought everyone else wanted him to be, because in his videos and photos he never looked comfortable. But as his career progressed, Jobs set a new standard—his standard: a black mock turtle neck sweater, jeans, and sneakers. This became part of the Steve Jobs brand. His presentation style was clunky at best, but he was a thought leader, and for many, the inspiration of the computer revolution. Jobs understood that it was more important to relate to his audience than it was to impress them with the way he looked or spoke.

Okay, I mentioned that Steve Jobs wasn't the best presenter. I feel like I should explain my comment. I have created cadence maps of his presentations, and most of them are executed, let's say, a bit choppy. However, when you are announcing the iMac or the iPhone, you can be clunky and get away with it. Jobs was just Jobs on that huge stage. I think it's funny to hear people say they are trying to present in the "Steve Jobs style." When I ask them what that style is, they usually say something like, "You know, casual and loose."

Nobody knew more about Apple Computer than Jobs. Nobody was more passionate about Apple than Jobs. Only Steve Jobs presented like Steve Jobs. It wasn't really a technique or style. It was just his way of showing off how amazing he thought Apple was and how he felt that the smartest people in the world were Apple people.

Steve Jobs always projected a level of confidence implying that Apple was WAY ahead of any competitor. They were the innovators of our time, and we didn't need to worry about what would come out next. They were already working on it. That attitude became a huge part of the Apple brand.

Your appearance and your attitude will set the stage for your presentation. If you are presenting to a group of scientists or engineers, and you show up in a tux, they probably won't hear a word you say. They'll spend most of your presentation time trying to figure out why you're dressed like that. Conversely, if you are presenting to a business group, you need to be dressed professionally, or they'll wonder who you think you are coming in wearing a plaid shirt and shorts.

Early in my career, I was working for the State of Utah Small Business Development Center. I was a senior in college and was called on to work with local small businesses to help them formulate marketing plans and set up systems for promoting their businesses. During my summer semester, a client came to the center asking for marketing support on a venture he was about to launch. He was planning on building a storage unit on the west side of Ogden city. He wanted to get some cheap research done before he moved ahead.

Since summer semester meant warm weather, I wore shorts and a t-shirt to the class I attended right before meeting with him. One of the University professors was with me, and the client turned to the professor during the meeting and said, "Um, do you have anyone older or more experienced that could work with me? I am not sure how he could help me." Yes, I was sitting three feet from him when he said that. The professor assured him that I was one of the best consultants in the program and that he would be taken care of. And then the biggest slap in the face of all, the professor said, "Don't worry, I'll check over his work before you see it." I was shocked at first but then determined to prove him wrong. I spent the next fifteen minutes interviewing him about his project, and following every question I asked, he responded to the professor, not me.

As you can imagine, I was determined to show this guy that I knew what I was doing and that he shouldn't have treated me that way. I went to work and engaged students from three marketing classes in the research. In a nutshell, the research showed that if he built a storage unit where he was planning, it would fail miserably. There were two other units within five miles and they were operating below half capacity. There were no future plans for home building locally because the land was unsuitable for development.

When we met back at the SBA center, I was dressed in a suit and was ready to just impress this guy to death with my knowledge of his project. I was so proud to tell him that we just saved him from a failing venture. The presentation went great. With every point of research I presented, I could see on his face that we had blown his mind. At the end of the presentation, I said, "As you can see, the feasibility of your project working at this location is very low. I would look for a new location with more potential development in the future."

We turned the lights on and he looked at me and said, "Wow. I wasn't expecting that." I was as proud as could be, until he made his next remark. "I wasn't sure you knew what you were doing, so I went ahead and bought the land and we broke ground last week. Am I in trouble?" This comment he said directly to me, not the professor, and I felt horrible that my initial impression gave him doubts about my ability. Needless to say, his project unfortunately failed.

When you conduct research on your audience, it's so important to take into account your appearance and the attitude with which you approach them when you present. You won't have long to earn their trust. Your objective should always be to create a level of harmony and trust with your audience as quickly as possible.

Tactics:

- Present as *you* present. Don't try to be someone else, because you can't sustain that act.

- Prepare for your first impression; you won't have a second chance.

- Conduct some research on your audience and try to meet their expectations.

Practice—It's More Skill Than Talent

The gift of gab. You probably know someone with this gift. For some, it's the ability to speak to a group of people off the cuff. It does require a level of knowledge about the topic, but more importantly, it requires confidence in your ability to communicate that knowledge. Most of these people have an archive of stories and examples to draw upon. For others, it's the ability to flat out BS your way through any topic!

Many people have a natural skill to speak and present, but I think if you were to dig into their past, they've probably been cultivating that talent over the years without even realizing it by speaking to their church congregations, presenting reports at school, or giving business presentations, just to name a few examples. In most cases, I believe success is 30% talent and 70% practice.

Presenting is very much like golf to me. I am not a great golfer. Actually, I was before I really started playing it and realized that you were supposed to count EVERY shot! Who does that? I always told people to put my handicap down as a 10. After playing with a client who took me under his wing for over eight years and playing in a men's league every Thursday for those eight years, I eventually got to a real 10 handicap. It literally took me years to achieve, and because I no longer play as much, my handicap has deteriorated simply due to the lack of practice.

Being able to pick up a club and hit the ball is only the tip of the iceberg in golf. For years, it seemed that the more I played, the worse I got. My handicap shot to an 18 and stayed there for nearly three seasons. I almost gave up the game and would have, if it weren't for my stubborn client who kept me playing. I also learned a very valuable lesson at this time: you can't buy a golf game. It only comes through practice—and a lot of it. I also learned that it is very important to practice the right way. If you practice bad habits, you'll get better at the bad habits and almost cement those habits into place. I ended up taking lessons to relearn how to hold the club, where to stand, and how to swing. These were things I thought I already knew. After all, in my mind, I was a 10 handicap for years. After breaking my game down and starting over, I gradually got better and better. A benchmark day in my golf life was at Sand Hollow Resort in Hurricane, Utah on the 13th hole of the Championship Course—a spectacular golf course.

I pulled out my driver, and my golf buddy said, "There's no way you'll keep that ball in play with your driver." I thought to myself, "Well, it's only one ball, and it'll be funny." He said, "You realize that you'll have to land that ball on that three-foot patch of grass at the top of that massive sand trap and then pray that it stops before it rolls off the back into the 200 foot canyon, right?" I pounded the shot and it hit right in the middle of that three-foot patch of grass. It bounced onto the green and stopped about 20 feet from the pin.

Once he got back to his feet from about passing out, he said, "I couldn't do that in a million shots." A few minutes later, I sunk that 20-foot putt with a double break for the luckiest eagle of my life. My golf mentor turned to me and said, "Wow, if you really practice, you might actually be able to play this game someday." That didn't seem like a compliment at the time.

My purpose in relating this golf analogy is to help you realize that there is always room for improvement through deeper knowledge and persistent practice. Learn all you can about presenting by watching experts speak and by reading how-to books. Don't be afraid to get real input on your techniques, and don't be too proud to admit when you need to work on something. It may be the only way you'll identify things that will make you better. You may find that you're not currently as good at presenting as you thought you were. That's okay, just figure out what you need to work on and practice it.

Getting in front of people at every opportunity will help you cultivate your talent into a valuable skill. Learning how to practice is very important, and committing to the art is a big step in the right direction. If you don't get the opportunity to speak often, build presentations on topics you're passionate about and practice them at home. You don't need to have an audience to practice. Call it your driving range. Get out and just hit balls. You're creating muscle memory and practicing techniques that you'll need one day. Remember, there isn't a shortcut. To get better at presenting, you need to put in the practice time.

I've heard of a new trend that friend groups are doing that I think is amazing. One night a month they get together for a potluck dinner, and two to four people give a 10-minute presentation on a topic they are passionate about. *(I think one of the rules is that it can't be about a multi-level marketing opportunity.)* The next month, they draw names out of a hat and it's someone else's turn. This is an amazing way to practice in the comfort of friends who will champion you and give you real feedback. They may laugh at you but only because they love you. Knowing that it will soon be their turn will keep them realistic. This is exactly like getting off the driving range and onto the real golf course. Nothing beats really playing the game.

Tactics:

- Identify elements of presenting that you want to improve.

- Volunteer to present when you get the opportunity.

- Build and practice presentations at home—even if it's without an audience.

- Start a presentation group with your friends. Practice!

Perception is Everything

When you present, you will project an impression to your audience. It will happen very quickly, and you will want their perception to be one that you can work with for the duration of the presentation.

At an event for Blue Cross Blue Shield, I was managing the multimedia for the opening session's emcees. They were two of their own salespeople, whom everyone absolutely loved. They were a little corny and just all-around good guys, but in no way were they professional emcees. They came out in big fur boots and did the opening as a skit of "Hans and Franz" from an old Saturday Night Live episode. Clunky and irreverent would be the only words to describe it, but because everyone knew and loved these two clowns, the audience was laughing hysterically and really enjoyed it. At the end of their skit they introduced their keynote speaker. He was a professional business speaker, and I'm sure he cost them a pretty penny. After being introduced, he came out on stage, and the audience gave him the typical welcome applause.

The first thing that came out of his mouth was, "Well, I was a little nervous to speak to you, but after watching those two bozos, I figured it couldn't get any worse than that." A hush fell across the audience and he never got the room back on his side.

It's very dangerous to make blind assumptions in front of your audience. Your reputation is very fragile at this point. When your audience doesn't know you, your background, or your experience, be very cautious about creating an early perception in a negative place from which you can't recover.

Establishing your position as a credible source or a capable partner early in the presentation will help you build equity with the audience. In any presentation, cultivating trust with the audience is important to help you guide them toward your objective. Treat them as part of your team. If they perceive you as a threat or competitor, they'll treat you that way; their posture will become closed and they will be projecting a defensive attitude. Once the audience goes on the defense, turning them is a daunting task.

Tactics:

- Be what they expect, and then build into someone they respect.

- Never take uneducated risks or create an enemy from the stage.

- Make it a point to cultivate trust with your audience; they are not an opponent.

Controlling and Leveraging Emotion

As a communications agency in Salt Lake City, Utah, Penna Powers secured a contract with the Utah Department of Transportation in its Traffic Safety division. The goal of the campaign was to reduce automobile fatalities statewide. The agency pitched a concept of "Zero Fatalities—A goal we can all live with." At first, the engineers at UDOT rejected the concept saying it was an unachievable goal. In an attempt to convince them of the campaign's potential, I took our lead strategist and Social Change Director, and we went out with our camera crew and interviewed people on the street. We asked them how many people they thought died on America's roads every year. Their numbers were all over the place. Most had no idea. Then we asked them how many they thought happened in Utah. Smaller numbers, but still all over the place. Then we asked them what a good goal for Utah would be?

Their responses ranged from "Half what it is now," to "I don't know, 1,000?" We got a little chuckle about it when one of them said, "Maybe just the bad drivers?" The amazing result in our research was the final question. We said, "Okay, if the goal in Utah is 100 or whatever you think, how many are you willing to have come from your family?" The reaction was stunning. Shock and horror would come over their faces and they would say, "Wait, zero from my family." In fact, one woman said, "That is a horrible thing to ask." Then, we asked them what the goal was for their family and they all said, zero. So, we asked them, "Shouldn't that be the state's goal as well?" And we got 100% yes answers. That very video strategy has been done in several states that have now adopted the Zero Goal for their traffic safety.

Utah did adopt the campaign, and it has been one of their primary objectives for years. Creating a campaign for this kind of effort requires exposing some fragile emotions. How do you convince a state full of people that they need to change their behavior, even though they all feel they are amazing drivers and that it will never happen to them?

One of the most powerful tactics we employed were presentations to parents with teens who were about to get their driver's license. Davis County School District made it mandatory that all students attend one of these presentations with a parent before they could get their license. Needless to say, a lot of parents were upset that they had to come to a presentation, especially when driver's education was taught in their school. Many felt like that should be enough. What we found was very interesting: Teens were more likely to set good driving habits if their parents were on the same page with them. These presentations put the parent and the student on the same page.

Our presentation took both the parent and the student through the top five behaviors that were killing people on the roads. Our presenters were trained to introduce the behavior and then share a tragic story about a teen who was killed because someone didn't respect the behavior. A thorough cadence was used to build the presentation and make sure our presenters didn't over-ignite the audience's emotions. But in this situation, emotion was a key tool in reaching our objective. Following the presentations, several parents wrote emails to UDOT exclaiming that the Zero Fatalities presentation not only changed their lives but may have even saved their lives. In presenter speak, we call that a success.

Using emotion is the glue that connects your message with the audience. Too much emotion creates an environment where you may not be able to manage the cadence, so keeping audience emotions under control is very important. If people start to get up and walk out because there is too much emotion, you'll lose the rest of the audience.

On the other hand, a presentation devoid of emotion is very hard for someone to get through. Engaging both sides of the brain is the best way to help an audience member connect with and internalize your message.

Tactics:

- Identify emotions that the audience will relate to.

- Think outside the box for ways to communicate your message with more emotion.

- Be sincere. Don't fake emotions as you present. If they aren't real, they won't be impactful.

*Give me six hours to chop down a tree and I will
spend the first four sharpening the axe.*

— *Abraham Lincoln*

Chapter 4
Preparation
The Cadence Chart System

The Outline

The concept of developing a presentation usually starts in
high school or college with an assignment to present a book
report or something. Using what we had been taught up
until that point, we wrote an outline for our presentation just
like we did to write the paper. In fact, we might have used
the same outline for the presentation. I am here to argue that
presentations are not papers and papers are not
presentations. Although you can use the written word to

move the emotions of a reader, in a presentation, you're dealing with multiple physical senses of the audience, and your physical body is also obviously engaged. When you only present with an outline method, it usually sounds like you just got up and read your paper.

Dynamic Presentation Outline

Presentations are much closer to acting than they are to writing a paper. If you've ever read a play manuscript, there are lines within the dialogue called blocking. These lines tell the reader what the actors should do or feel as they deliver their lines. This brings the written word to life, and your imagination puts the script into motion.

In high school, I competed in a state championship for a one-act play. I chose the Drowned Man scene from Neil Simon's, The Good Doctor as my material. As I read through the script, it instructed me to speak the lines with a British accent and act like I was drunk. Just reading this script would give you a little chuckle simply because of the scenario that's taking place. But add in a British accent, funny body language, the facial expressions of a drunk, timing, and the variable tones and volume as the lines are delivered, and it becomes a hilarious situation—completely engaging the audience and eliciting a lot of laughter. Not that it matters, but I won the competition, and even more importantly, I had people coming up to me for years asking me to please do it again, which meant it was memorable.

Presenting is more than just slamming a bunch of stories or information together and delivering them to a group of people. If you've ever sat through a poorly-planned presentation, you've experienced the pain of the just-get-through-it feeling. Putting a plan together doesn't need to be difficult or painstaking, but it will help organize your thoughts so your communication and message is consumable for your audience. I have spent three decades helping companies of all sizes develop their presentations. I have financed that learning curve and developed fool-proof planning tools that will make it easy to organize your thoughts, give you opportunities to plan beyond your information, and actually create an experience for your audience every time. With a dynamic outline you can simply split the page and add the desired dynamics you are trying to create on the right side of your outline. This is a simple yet effective way to take into account the emotions you are trying to manage during your presentation.

Dynamic Presentation Outline

Emotional Condition: *Department is upset with the new dress code policy.*
Audience: *Many have been with the company for over five years and this change makes them feel like the company isn't listening or doesn't care what they want.*

Content Outline

I: Restate new Dress Code Policy
 a. Read the new policy from the policy manual.
 b. Discuss who was involved in the creation of the new policy.
 c. Explain that the company didn't just decide one day to make the policy.

II: Why did this become policy?
 a. People are dressing too casually.
 b. Clients have mentioned that our "professionalism" is weakening.
 c. We want the company and our people to have a good, professional reputation.

III: What is the consequence for not following the policy?
 a. Three warnings from management.
 b. Third notice brings probation.
 c. Fourth notice is termination.

IV: What do we feel the outcome will be?
 a. We will "look" better and "perform" better.
 b. We'll stand out from our competition.
 c. Our clients will feel that we are more professional and be willing to pay more for our services.

V: Why do we all need to adhere to the policy?
 a. This only works if we're all on board.
 b. We don't want this policy to just be for our client-facing staff. Professionalism impacts all of us.
 c. This will become part of our "Brand."

VI: How can you be involved in future discussions.
 a. Submit your willingness to be on an HR committee.
 b. Leadership team selects staff members to join committees to engage their input.
 c. We want everyone in the company to feel heard, and we try very hard to make decisions that impact you for the better.

VII: Answer any questions.
 a. Assess if there are any unanswered questions.
 b. BUT DO NOT PUT UP A "QUESTIONS" SLIDE.

Dynamic Outline

I: Show them that this change has been made and isn't going away. (Authority)

 a. Defuse the opinion that management made the call in a silo.

II: Educate them and clarify decision points.

III: Clearly explain expectations and consequences. This is not a drill or a joke.

IV: Bring their emotions back up by telling them how much better and more valuable they will be, how the company will be better.

V: Make them feel that EVERYONE is involved in this new policy. Not just management.

VI: Make them feel empowered to impact changes in the company by being more involved.

VII: Give them a chance to ask questions, but try to keep the group calm and motivated.

Tactics:

- Use a dynamic presentation outline to fuse the information you're trying to communicate with the emotion you're trying to generate.

- Blocking will add emotion and action to your presentation

Define Key Presentation Elements

The effort you put into planning your presentation will pay off if you go into it with the right attitude. The more you know, the less you guess—and guessing is expensive. Putting a plan together is much like building a house. I use the home building analogy quite often because it helps people clearly see the different phases on a physical and relatable level.

Blueprint—Planning documents: an outline, dynamic outline, or Cadence Chart

Foundation—Primary objectives for the presentation

Framing—The elements and topics used to build your story

Electrical—Connecting the elements or topics to tie the presentation together

Design and finish work—The visuals used to communicate your messages

Decor—This is you. This is the key element that makes the whole presentation work. You are the personality of the presentation.

If you've ever seen a home that someone built without a good plan, you'll understand why a blueprint is so important. Whether it's a basic outline or a dynamic tool, get all of the components down on a document that you can follow as you build. The foundation of the house is your primary objective. What are you are trying to accomplish with the presentation? After you answer that question, ask yourself this one: What are you really trying to accomplish with the presentation? Many times, we focus on what we assume the objective is when in reality, the true objective is just below the surface of an assumed one. So, in the analogy of building a house, the true objective is the base material supporting the foundation. It is very important to make sure the material under the foundation is firm; otherwise, the whole structure will fail. Once you have identified the true objective, your foundation is the structure that will hold your entire presentation. In the foundation, try to identify the main topics you'll be covering. Adding an additional room after the home is built is possible but very difficult if it wasn't part of the plan. If you have more than one objective, try to boil them down into a tight grouping so you can organize your presentation based on those objectives.

For example, if you're making a presentation to your sales team about how your company sales numbers are down, you're actually making a presentation to motivate them to work harder and set goals to improve. The sales numbers are what the presentation is about, but motivating them to set goals and improve performance is your base objective.

Once the foundation is in place, start framing your structure. At this stage, gather your elements and topics and organize them into a basic structure. Use Post-it notes, index cards, or a white board to identify them, and then assemble them into a framework on a table or a white board. This will help you get them in the right place before you start building. As the framework is built, begin identifying the key elements that you'll need to create a flow to your presentation. This is the electrical system of your project. As you build the structure, you need to tie in the components that will help you move through your information. After these critical elements are in place, you are ready to assemble your presentation.

The design and finish work phase is where you assemble all of the elements and put the slides together. The overall design of your presentation should align with your audience. Questions like, "What would they be comfortable with?" "How much content would they like to see?" and "How 'designed' is it?" will help to ensure that you are building the presentation with your audience in mind. Decide what special features you need to add to achieve your objective. Do you need video, animations, diagrams? Media elements can help communicate your message with greater impact. Exercise caution to not let them dominate your presentation and overpower you. Also remember, if you put something on a slide and feel like you might say to the audience, "I know you can't read or see this, but . . ." please rethink it. It's like building a staircase that doesn't go anywhere. It doesn't actually do anything for anyone.

The decor of your presentation is YOU. Your personality is critical in making your presentation come to life. The impact of a presentation is a combination of a well-structured and well-designed tool and the personality that you as a presenter add to bring the presentation to life. It's a little like the difference between a house and a home. Without the presenter, it's just information.

Tactics:

- Think of your presentation like building a home. You need a blueprint or plan in order to get it right.

- Identify your real objectives and build on them.

- Choose media elements wisely. They can help or hurt your presentation.

- Be YOU. Allow your personality to bring the presentation to life.

Landmines and Easter Eggs

One of the most creative and strategic tools a presenter can use are what I call "Easter eggs." This is an element of the presentation that is hidden from the direct flow of the presentation but is available if the presenter needs it. Landmines are topics that may create danger or opposition for the presenter. If you've done your research, you might uncover a topic that is sensitive or even volatile to your objective. For example, if the audience is unresponsive to the presentation, the presenter may have a slide positioned after their closing slide with a testimonial video, impactful animation, data chart, or other multimedia component that clarifies and defends your position. It is something that the presenter would not normally use in their presentation and will often go unused, but it waits for the perfect opportunity to come to the rescue if needed.

I was working with a small credit union that was trying to open a branch office inside of the Franklin Covey complex located in Salt Lake City, Utah. The president of the credit union was very passionate about making it happen, but he didn't think they had a chance because they were too small. I built them a great presentation, but he cautiously kept saying, "I am so excited to present this, but I'm afraid they'll think we're too small to pull it off." He was obviously intimidated by the size of Franklin Covey. I felt that it was going to be the one thing that might lose the deal for them, whether it was a real issue or not. Mainly because HE felt it was an issue. So I asked him if he knew anyone who worked at Franklin Covey. He said, "The reason we want to go after it is because one of our board members was one of the founders of Franklin Covey." I asked him if I could meet with this individual and ask them some questions on video. They all agreed, and while I was interviewing him, I asked, "One of the concerns we have is that the management team at Franklin Covey will think we're too small to support and service Franklin Covey. Do you feel that is an issue?" His response put a big smile on my face. He said, "Heavens no, they work with one client at a time just like the credit union does. When it comes to one-to-one service, they get it." I put that video as an Easter egg in the presentation and cautioned the president, "If they don't raise the topic as an issue—DO NOT PLAY THIS VIDEO." I knew it was going to kill him to not play it, but I explained that if it wasn't an issue, and he showed the video, he'd make it one.

The day of the presentation there were about 20 people in the audience, and Franklin Covey's vice president was sitting in the middle of the pack. The presentation was going great, and then, to my utter astonishment, the vice president triggered the landmine: "This is all great and you look like a really impressive company, but what makes you think you can handle a corporation of our size?" I about died. The president looked over at me, and I just smiled. He said, "I am glad you asked that question," and hit the Easter egg button. When the video stopped playing, the vice president chuckled and said, "I am sorry I interrupted you. We won't ask any more stupid questions." The president of the credit union could barely contain his emotions as he finished the presentation. Work to open the branch started soon thereafter.

Easter eggs are incredibly powerful tools, and they can work for you, or if poorly executed, against you. Most presentation software will provide the presenter with the ability to jump to a screen and return quickly without disrupting the flow of the presentation. These tools should be used only in situations that require a boost. If the Easter egg is meant to overcome an obstacle, like in my previous example, the worst thing you can do is expose the issue. If the prospect doesn't bring it up, leave it hidden.

Tactics:

- Prepare for unexpected landmines in your presentation with additional information to support your objective.

- Never introduce a weakness or issue that could put doubt in your audience's mind.

- Master your presentation software to utilize its capabilities.

- Testimonials are one of the most powerful Easter eggs available. They are hard to argue with, and they usually mute an issue of concern.

Phrasing vs. Memorizing

Memorizing a presentation is a safe way to guarantee that you'll deliver the message you've planned to deliver. But memorizing can often come off a bit canned and impersonal. If you give a presentation several times, you will naturally perfect the timing and delivery. This is much different from just memorizing something verbatim. Connecting with the audience is critical during a presentation. If you memorize your presentation, you won't be able to adjust it if your audience disconnects from you for any reason. Also, I have found that many times when people memorize their presentation verbatim, they inevitably hit a pothole and/or have a "brain cramp" and that can cause full on panic before they find their way back to the road. Phrasing is a much better way to remember your thoughts and make your message more natural and less rigid. Phrasing is a term I use that helps presenters avoid verbal tics while embedding their presentation firmly in their mind. Once your presentation is complete, print your slides out four to a page. Instead of memorizing your whole presentation, identify key phrases within it and write them next to the slide and just take a walk. Carry your slide deck with you and just talk through the phrases that will help you connect your thoughts through the presentation. I wouldn't do this in front of a mirror because you may lose focus on what you're saying versus how you look saying it. Just walk around your house or neighborhood and talk about the slides using your key phrases as the focus. You'll be amazed how it will help you communicate better and smoother as well as relieve the tension of knowing what to say next.

While I was working with one of our teams that were about to present to a potential client, I realized that two of the team members were having serious issues articulating their information. They kept saying things like, "Oh, I won't actually say that," or "Let me say that again." The presentation was the next morning, and I knew if this was how the presentation went, the client would run for the hills. I stopped the rehearsal and said, "Hey, I think we're pushing this too hard. I want you to take copies of the slides you'll be presenting and after you have dinner, put on your walking shoes and just go for an hour walk and talk about your slides. Don't memorize anything. You are a professional in your field, and the words are getting in the way of your ability to communicate." The next morning, we met one more time to just run through it. The improvement was remarkable. When their slides came up, they started talking about the information as if we were discussing it over lunch. I was incredibly relieved, and we actually won the client. Phrasing will help you put your thoughts into a loose framework. It will also help you avoid verbal crutches like "Um," "Uh," "Like," or any number of other connectors that find their way between your thoughts as you speak and you'll find that you are much more comfortable and articulate.

Tactics:

- Avoid memorizing your entire presentation if at all possible.

- Practice phrasing your thoughts to help your brain deliver them naturally and without interruption.

- Print your presentation and get comfortable with the phrases that will connect your slides with your message.

- Don't just talk to your audience; communicate with them.

Visuals or No Visuals

I love using visuals because they engage the audience's mind on a level that presenters typically can't do with their body and voice alone. Comedians typically have an amazing skill using their bodies as part of their delivery instead of slides. As a presenter, learning how to present and interact with visuals is very important. Too many presenters simply put every word on the screen. That makes the audience wonder why you didn't just email them the file. It also tends to pull the attention of the audience away from the presenter. The danger of the presenter just turning into an audio track is very high. Striking a balance of strong, impactful images that don't overpower the presenter is an art form. I always remind myself of this phrase when I'm building visuals: "Just because it's possible, doesn't mean it's practical." Good photographs, animations, videos, and other assets in your presentation can add a great deal of professionalism. Bad ones cause confusion and pain for your audience. I have always said that bad animations are worse than no animations. This applies to all assets used in your presentation.

In some presentations, visuals are not allowed or even possible. In that case, the presenter assumes the role of both speaker and visuals. Facial expressions, body positioning, eye contact, vocal tone, voice and volume fluctuation, etc., all play a more important role without the support of visuals. Also, the skill of storytelling plays an even more significant role without visuals. Stories will help the presenter engage the audience on an emotional level by bringing their imagination into the moment.

Where do you get your visuals? Well, in the past it was very difficult to find the perfect image for your presentation. With the Internet, those days are long gone. However, this does bring up an important subject. As I mentioned earlier, using images that do not belong to you can be dicey at best. If you are using rights-protected artwork, you must acquire the right to use it. It's very tempting to just snag images, videos, and animations off the Internet. Be sensitive to work that people have produced and make sure you get permission or rights to the visuals before you use them. Usually that permission will come from purchasing a license to use it. If not, you'll have to hunt the owner down to get permission.

Tactics:

- Visuals help take the presentation to a higher level of impact if the they assist the presenter in validating or supporting a comment.

- Find a balance between your visuals and yourself. Don't let your visuals overpower you.

- Be careful and sensitive with the assets you use in your presentation. Get the rights and permissions before you use them.

Practice Being Human

After years of working with presenters in all walks of life, I've come to understand a very interesting phenomenon: People tend to like presentations given by people that they like. Whether they like the presenter or not is usually determined in the first five minutes of the presentation. Sure, you can turn the audience around if they don't initially like you, but chances are they will watch for things in your presentation that validate their initial opinion of you.

When our agency was conducting driver's ed. safety parents' nights for the Utah Department of Transportation, I had the opportunity to take my 15-year old son to one of the presentations. Stacy Allen was delivering the presentation to a group of about 150 people in our town. Stacy had given this presentation hundreds of times to groups of anywhere between 5 to 500 people. She knew the information forward and backward, and she is an amazing presenter. She and I put the presentation together years earlier, and we had trained dozens of presenters on how to deliver it. On this night, I didn't tell Stacy that I was coming to the presentation. I just wanted to observe her style and see how the audience was receiving the presentation. I sat with my son about ten rows back on the left side of the stage. Stacy has a magnetic personality and was able to engage the audience in minutes. Then, something very funny happened. She looked over and saw me. Instead of just continuing on with the presentation like I assumed she would, she pointed at me and said to the audience, "Hey! Oh yikes, my boss is here! Now I'm really nervous." The audience broke into laughter, she jumped right back into the presentation, and the whole group was eating out of her hands the rest of the evening. She showed that she was human, let them see the real Stacy, and it endeared them to her.

Tactics:

- Being human and relatable will help you cultivate a real relationship with your audience.

- Be sensitive to your audience and stay away from topics or ideas that may cause them to form a negative opinion of you.

- You have five minutes to win the audience's initial opinion of you. Make it count.

The Closing Slide

This, admittedly, is one of my biggest pet peeves. Nothing tells the audience that you're a novice or that you are literally leaning on your presentation slides as a crutch like a closing screen that has the word, "Questions," or even worse, "The End" on it.

Don't be afraid to put up a visual or quote that can prompt you to say, "Okay folks, that's the end of what I was planning to present. Do you have any questions?" without actually showing a giant question mark on the screen. This will give the audience the impression that you are in control of the visuals: you are presenting, not the slides. Sometimes I wonder why it freaks me out so much, but I feel that putting up a slide like that at the end of a presentation absolutely destroys any momentum you might have. This is the time when you should be focused on the cadence of your presentation reaching a higher impact. Don't drop it on its head!

Almost every time we do a workshop on presenting where we film the participants doing their micro-presentation, they put a questions screen at the end. I think it's mainly because they aren't sure how to visually close their presentation. At this point, I try to help them understand that as they improve as a presenter, they won't feel the need for an actual closing slide with the word "Questions?" on it.

The Cadence Chart System

While I was developing presentations for some clients in the early 1990s, I found it clunky and frustrating to help them figure out how to organize their thoughts into an impactful presentation that achieved their goals. I sat down and interviewed them. I did research. I interviewed their clients. Usually by that time, I was ready to build the presentation. I felt that I knew just what to do. In reality, it was just my opinion of what to do. Over time, I wanted to validate that my opinion and strategy was accurate. I struggled with how to convey my strategy to them in a way that they could see the whole presentation at once.

Years ago, my wife and I went to a movie. It was her turn to pick, so we went to Sleepless in Seattle. YIKES! I tried to conceal the kid in me who was screaming out, "Oh no, not a romance movie!" But she had suffered through many action movies, and it was her turn to pick. That said, I have a confession: I am a movie buff. I love movies—yes, even romances. I love movies because they are an escape for my brain, but it wasn't on this day. As I was watching the movie, I kept going back to my problem of how to validate a presentation strategy, and then out of the blue, it hit me like a ton of bricks. The content of any presentation is like the elements of a movie. Movie makers use storylines, plots, characters, sound effects, music, and scenery to control the cadence or rhythm of the movie. Hollywood has figured this out. In fact, fast forward with me to 2019. Bradley Cooper was being interviewed on a talk show about his movie A Star is Born. The interviewer asked, "You let the film breathe; you let us breathe; Was that your intent?" Bradley's response validated my suspicion of 25 years. "Absolutely, I love movies. Movies have provided me, as I am sure most of you, a lot of healing and inspiration over the years. I think by being a student of it and having people like David O. Russell and Clint Eastwood be so open about their process. It's all *rhythm* too, as a love story it should breathe." That was it. Whether movie directors realize what they are doing or not, being able to move the audience dynamically in a rhythm is critical to the success of a movie.

After Sleepless in Seattle ended, I was so excited about this idea that I went back to my office and grabbed a legal pad and pencil and went back to the theater. This time, I was drawing a timeline across the page as I watched. As the tempo or action in the movie would increase or decrease, I would take the curve up or down. When I finished, I was in shock. I saw the movie in one glance. I watched the movie again and this time I put markers and events that caused the shift in rhythm or cadence. When I was done, I sat there as the folks were sweeping up popcorn, and I realized that I had found it. *(And I had almost memorized the movie.)*

Why did I choose the word 'cadence' to define my process? In my youth I played the drums and I was taught that the cadence was the powerful underlying element of every song. The Merriam-Webster dictionary agreed with me—Cadence —1.b. the beat, time, or measure of rhythmical motion or activity.

That was it! I went back to my office and took out the sort cards for the client's presentation I was working on. I organized and grouped them by their impact value. I created a crude, hand-drawn Cadence Chart and placed the cards in their position. Everything fell into place. I spent the rest of the night making a digital version of the Cadence Chart and presented it to the client the next morning. Once I had explained the concept, they were blown away. This was an invention that would change my career forever. I practiced charting movies for years. I needed to learn how to distinguish the components of the story and break it down visually. I realized that it wasn't the theme or genre of the movie that impacted the cadence, it was the emotion that the movie was generating at each moment. After years of practicing it, I can't go to a movie without cadencing it in my head. And, by the way, if I just ruined your movie-going experience forever, I'm truly sorry. But you'll be a much better presenter for it. I think it's a great trade-off, plus it is so interesting to view movies from a new perspective. So how do you practice recognizing and identifying a cadence? Go to movies, plays, musicals, and of course presentations, and map them out. I will show you my process of developing Cadence Charts and a few examples over the next few pages.

Why Does It Work?

Everyone is unique in so many ways. However, there are certain human characteristics that are more common among us. I am a big fan of the Marvel movies. Okay, I don't *(always)* sleep in Iron Man pajamas but I really enjoy the movies. When I bump into someone who says, "Yeah, they're not my cup of tea," I simply can't understand it. But that is what makes us human. We all have different tastes. I loved the movie Oh Brother, Where Art Thou. In fact, my wife told our kids that their prospective spouses needed to watch that movie with us. If they didn't like it or didn't get it, they had better move on. We love that kind of humor. On the other hand, we watched The Royal Tenenbaums and when it ended, I said to my wife, "I feel like I'm the victim of a bad practical joke." I couldn't believe my ears when someone would tell me it was one of their favorite movies.

Consider the Harry Potter movies, when the theater opened for another Harry Potter, the line of people who really wanted to see the movie was a mile long. They were consumed by it. Every second of that movie was just delicious to them. What made that happen? They were fans. They had invested in either watching the movies or reading the books. They love Harry Potter and they all love it for different reasons. Therefore, it was important for the movie makers to keep the flow that J.K. Rowling had created in her books, at least as closely as they could.

The movie takes people on a journey, an emotional journey with highs and lows. There are parts that built the storyline, and parts that just entertained us, parts that make us cry, and parts that make us jump with fright. All done with music, sound effects, visual effects, and storylines.

Now consider a movie without the cadence figured out—the scene opens with a guy sitting on a couch in his office and you watch him eat a bag of Cheetos for 20 minutes—you'd bail and ask for your money back. Conversely, if the movie started with a planet blowing up and for the next 45 minutes, things kept blowing up on the screen, you would have a very different emotion, but your reaction would be the same: you'd get up and leave, asking for your money back.

There is a balance required for us to get and stay engaged. Too much or too little is uncomfortable, and we often mentally shut down.

In live presentations, the presenter is the actor, the content is the storyline, and the audience is the target. The Cadence Chart helps the presenter organize the storyline with a balanced tempo that creates the cadence for their presentation. It helps the presenter move away from the content and focus on their audience, helping them deliver their message in a pattern that will be more consumable.

This is the Cadence Chart of Steve Job's presentation announcing the iPhone in 2007.

Presentation Cadence Chart
Steve Jobs | Apple Computer 2007 iPhone Announcement

Structure breakdown

A Cadence Chart is designed with several areas of focus. The objective of the cadence is to create a visual, skeletal structure that exposes the desired emotion the presenter is trying to manage during their presentation. If a presenter can master the art of using emotions, they will be able to deliver their presentation in a way that the audience will relate to more deeply.

Cadence Chart—The Cadence Chart is broken down into four quadrants and is spread over a timeline that is represented by percent of time. Each presentation will be a different length. This will help you determine if you need to add or delete parts of your presentation to make it effective in the allotted time. It is unwise to prepare a one-hour presentation and then try to cram it into a 30-minute window. You can use the cadence to evaluate your content and determine what needs to be deleted or added to keep the cadence effective.

Emotional baseline—The emotional baseline is the dotted line that spans the presentation. This line is set by evaluating the pre-existing level of emotion the audience may have about you and your subject. This isn't their happy line. It is

Level of excitement / interest / emotion

Low   High

Presentation Title

Emotional Baseline

Keyframe Trigger

Cadence flow

Topic elements and blocking

Desired emotion comments

Percentage of time

Stories

Objective

Objective: Desired outcome of the presentation

0 10 20 30 40 50 60 70 80 90 100

determined by their expectation of the presentation. For example, if your topic is training, the emotional line might be lower and your objective is to create higher spikes to keep the audience interested and engaged. This gauge needs to be set with more room at the top of the chart to allow for the presentation to move into a higher emotional state as it progresses. Most presenters aren't trying to "bring the audience down." However, there is sound logic in trying to cross this line several times during the presentation. Your presentation always starts at this line. If you try to move the audience high above it and keep them there, chances are you'll burn them out if your presentation is long. It is very difficult to continue to move that emotion line upward without them feeling over-stimulated. Conversely, if you move them below the line too deep or for too long, you may never get them back to a positive point to close your presentation and hit your objective.

Keyframe triggers—Keyframe triggers are markers in your presentation where you will be shifting the topic. These keyframes, located at the top of the chart, help you manage how much time you spend within a specific topic. Once you have the keyframe trigger identified, you'll be able to determine what content you can develop within it for each topic and remain on cadence.

Within the keyframe triggers, it is helpful to put in transition comments to help you remember how you'll transition to the new topic. A brief comment with the connector identified can be put on the map above the baseline. Below the baseline, you can put comments that spell out what your objective is within that keyframe period. The transitions are critical pieces of the presentation. If they are not smooth and seamless, they appear to be staccato breaks and can disrupt the cadence dramatically. One of the best transition tools is telling a story. It is important that the story is well-positioned for the transition. It must be placed at a point that it can seamlessly tie back into the cadence of the presentation with the stories resolution.

Stories—I am convinced that a key factor in a successful presentation is when the presenter is aware of, and even targeting, the 7-year-old inside every member of their audience. Everyone in that room was 7-years-old at some point, and the 7-year-old is generally driven by emotion much more than they are by facts. Stories that don't engage emotions are just a bunch of well-organized words. Good presenters perfect the ability of using stories to move their cadence and can actually move the cadence up or down with them. If the topic is moving the audience's emotions up too fast, a story can be used to calm the tempo a bit. It will help disconnect the logical thought processes and engage their imagination. In the case where the audience is not moving, the presenter can inject a story that can help engage that emotion to bring the audience back into their cadence. We'll go into detail on storytelling in the connection chapters later.

Document Landmines and Strategies

Within the Cadence Chart, you can identify potential landmines that may disrupt or even derail your presentation. Once you have targeted where the landmine might be, you strategically organize your content or plant Easter eggs to defend your presentation at that point on your timeline. You may not be able to identify all potential landmines, but if you can isolate the ones you can see, you'll be much better off. Be careful not to expose a weakness just because you're afraid it might be one. Your audience may not perceive it as a weakness until you expose it.

Adjusting the Cadence

Moving the cadence is done by employing a handful of basic techniques. In the movie or theatrical environment, directors use music, sound effects, or topic and scene transitions and dozens of other tactics to cause the shift. In a presentation, you'll have body movements, voice tone and volume, audiovisuals, stories, and topic changes that you can use to move the cadence. Simple adjustments can be made by pace and speed. Ironically, one of the most powerful tools is silence. Silence placed before a keyframe trigger will bring the audience to attention and allow the presenter to guide the cadence with their next sentence. Silence used in a story will amplify the emotion you are trying to generate. In a sad story, it will cause the audience to reflect deeper. In a happy story, it will increase their emotions more rapidly and raise the cadence at a faster rate.

Adjusting the cadence allows the presenter to control the room on a macro level. Every audience member will be moved in their own way, but even their individual reactions will cause others around them to adjust. The objective is to create a comfortable cadence that will keep the audience engaged and drive them to your desired objective or position.

Different Types of Presentations

How many different types of presentation are there? Well, that depends on what you're willing to call a presentation. Starting at the most basic and typically unrecognized presentations, you present every time you interact with another person at the bank, store, or fast food window. But let's push past those and focus on presentations where you, the presenter, have the floor or stage and are speaking to a group of more than your lunch squad. These can include sales pitches, training classes, business presentations, or lectures. In short, courtrooms, classrooms, conference rooms, and events.

Each of these would have a basic cadence template. Following are some examples of templates that you could start with. Each type of presentation has a different cadence pattern to achieve specific goals and move the audience in a specific way.

Presentation Cadence Samples

Lecture Template—This template is a base strategy for a lecture presentation. The primary objective is to actively guide the audience to a specific conclusion or understanding. Focus on key topics that will help keep the audience's attention and communicate your message. Bringing the audience into a singular position at the beginning will make it much easier to move the group.

Unless there is a need to motivate the audience, the fluctuation of the cadence doesn't need to be too turbulent. Subtle variations will usually hold the audience and keep them engaged. After all, they should be expecting a lecture and not a motivational speech.

A consistent rise in emotion at the end will help your audience feel they have received value and information from the lecture.

LECTURE | Presentation Cadence Chart

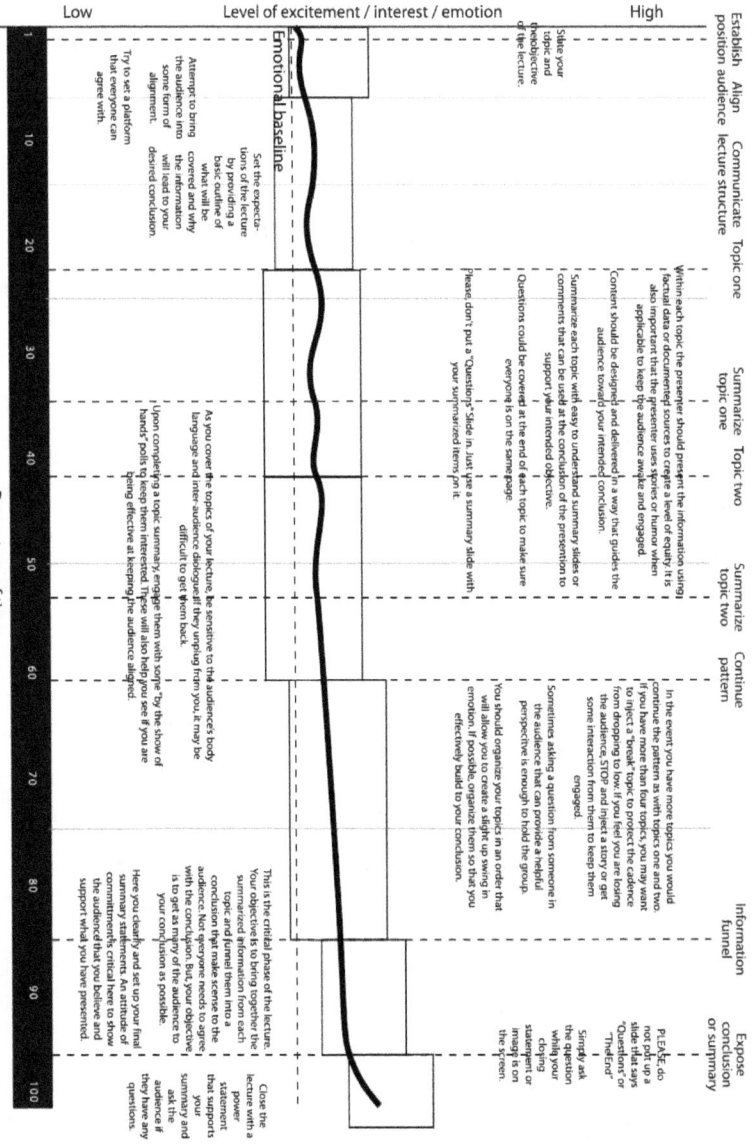

Level of excitement / interest / emotion — Low .... High

Percentage of time: 1 — 10 — 20 — 30 — 40 — 50 — 60 — 70 — 80 — 90 — 100

Emotional baseline

Column headers: Establish position audience | Align lecture structure | Communicate Topic one | Summarize topic one | Topic two | Summarize topic two | Continue pattern | Information funnel | Expose conclusion or summary

Establish position audience
Try to set a platform that everyone can agree with.

Align lecture structure
Attempt to bring the audience into some form of alignment. the information will lead to your desired conclusion.

Set the expectations of the lecture by providing a basic outline of what will be covered and why

Communicate Topic one
Within each topic the presenter should present the information using factual data or documented sources to create a level of equity. It is also important that the presenter uses stories or humor when applicable to keep the audience awake and engaged.

Content should be designed and delivered in a way that guides the audience toward your intended conclusion.

Questions could be covered at the end of each topic to make sure everyone is on the same page.

Please, don't put a "Question" Slide in. Just use a summary slide with your summarized items on it.

Summarize topic one
Summarize each topic with easy to understand summary slides or comments that can be used at the conclusion of the presentation to support your intended objective.

Upon completing a topic summary, engage them with some "by the show of hands" polls to keep them interested. These will also help you see if you are being effective at keeping the audience aligned.

Topic two
As you cover the topics of your lecture, be sensitive to the audience's body language and inter-audience dialog. If they unplug from you, it may be difficult to get them back.

Continue pattern
In the event you have more topics you would continue the pattern as with topics one and two. If you have more than four topics, you may want to inject a "break" topic to protect the cadence from dropping to low. If you are losing the audience, STOP and inject a story or get some interaction from them to keep them engaged.

Sometimes asking a question from someone in the audience that can provide a helpful perspective is enough to hold the group.

You should organize your topics in an order that will allow you to create a slight up swing in emotion. If possible, organize them so that you effectively build to your conclusion.

Information funnel
This is the critical phase of the lecture. Your objectives to bring together the summarized information from each topic and funnel them into a conclusion that make sense to the audience. Not everyone needs to agree with the conclusion. But your objective is to get as many of the audience to agree with your conclusion as possible.

Here you clearly and set up your final summary statements. An attitude of commitment is critical here to show the audience that you believe and support what you have presented.

Expose conclusion or summary
PLEASE do not put up a slide that says "Questions" or "The End"

Simply ask the question while your closing statement or image is on the screen.

Close the lecture with a power statement that supports your summary and ask the audience if they have any questions.

Sales Template—This template is a base strategy for a sales presentation. The primary objective is to impress the audience while demonstrating your ability to provide what they are looking for. Focus on creating alignments and building a feeling of what their future will look like and the relationship your company will cultivate. Set your objective based on what they are looking for. Do your research—don't assume you know what their hot buttons are.

The transitions should be smooth and the variation of the cadence fluid. Trying to get the cadence too high at any point in the sales template may push the client out of their comfort zone. You'll want to save some room for a ramp up of emotion and excitement for your closing.

Sales presentations are all about demonstrating the alignment between your organization and your potential client. It's important to find those alignments and assure potential clients that you're aware of them as well. They're looking for a teammate, so create a comfortable but attractive perception to win it.

SALES | Presentation Cadence Chart

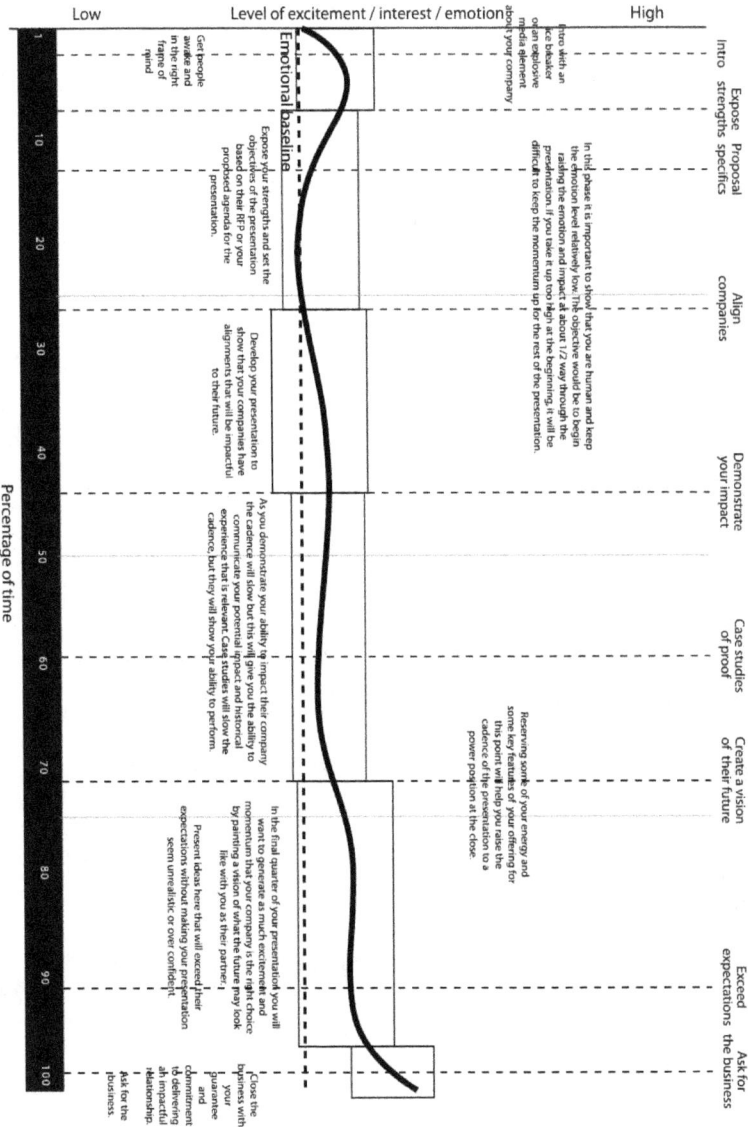

Level of excitement / interest / emotion — Low · High

Percentage of time — 1, 10, 20, 30, 40, 50, 60, 70, 80, 90, 100

Phases: Intro · Expose strengths specifics · Proposal specifics · Align companies · Demonstrate your impact · Case studies of proof · Create a vision of their future · Exceed expectations · Ask for the business

Emotional baseline

Intro with an ice breaker or an explosive media element about your company

In this phase it is important to show that you are human and keep the emotion level relatively low. The objective would be to begin raising the emotion and impact at about 1/2 way through the presentation. If you take it up too high at the beginning, it will be difficult to keep the momentum up for the rest of the presentation.

Get people awake and in the right frame of mind

Expose your strengths and set the objectives of the presentation based on their RFP or your proposed agenda for the presentation.

Develop your presentation to show that your companies have alignments that will be impactful to their future.

As you demonstrate your ability to impact their company the cadence will slow but this will give you the ability to communicate your potential impact and historical experience that is relevant. Case studies will slow the cadence, but they will show your ability to perform.

Receiving some of your energy and some key features of your offering for this point will help you raise the cadence of the presentation to a power position at the close.

In the final quarter of your presentation you will want to generate as much excitement and momentum that your company is the right choice by painting a vision of what the future may look like with you as their partner.

Present ideas here that will exceed their expectations without making your presentation seem unrealistic or over confident.

Close the business with your guarantee and commitment to delivering an impactful relationship. Ask for the business

Presenter Evolution

Training Template—This template is a base strategy for a training presentation. The number of sequences will depend on the amount of information being covered. The primary objective is to keep the momentum moving to avoid deep falls, as they are very difficult to recover from. A slight incline in overall emotion would be optimal to ensure participants leave the training in a better emotional state than they started.

Training presentations are unique because often the audience members may all have different emotions or opinions about the subject matter. Your job as the presenter is to keep the information moving at a rate where they can consume it while entertaining them enough to hold their attention and keep them engaged.

Gently ebbing and flowing around your emotional baseline will keep them engaged if the information is delivered in a compelling way. Using random spikes in the cadence will help reset them at a subtly higher level. Continue this pattern throughout your training and your results will be great.

TRAINING | Presentation Cadence Chart

Low   Level of excitement / interest / emotion   High

Emotional baseline

Percentage of time

1 · 10 · 20 · 30 · 40 · 50 · 60 · 70 · 80 · 90 · 100

Sequence labels: Intro · Topic launch · Topic summary transitional story · Topic launch · Topic summary transitional story · Summary motivation

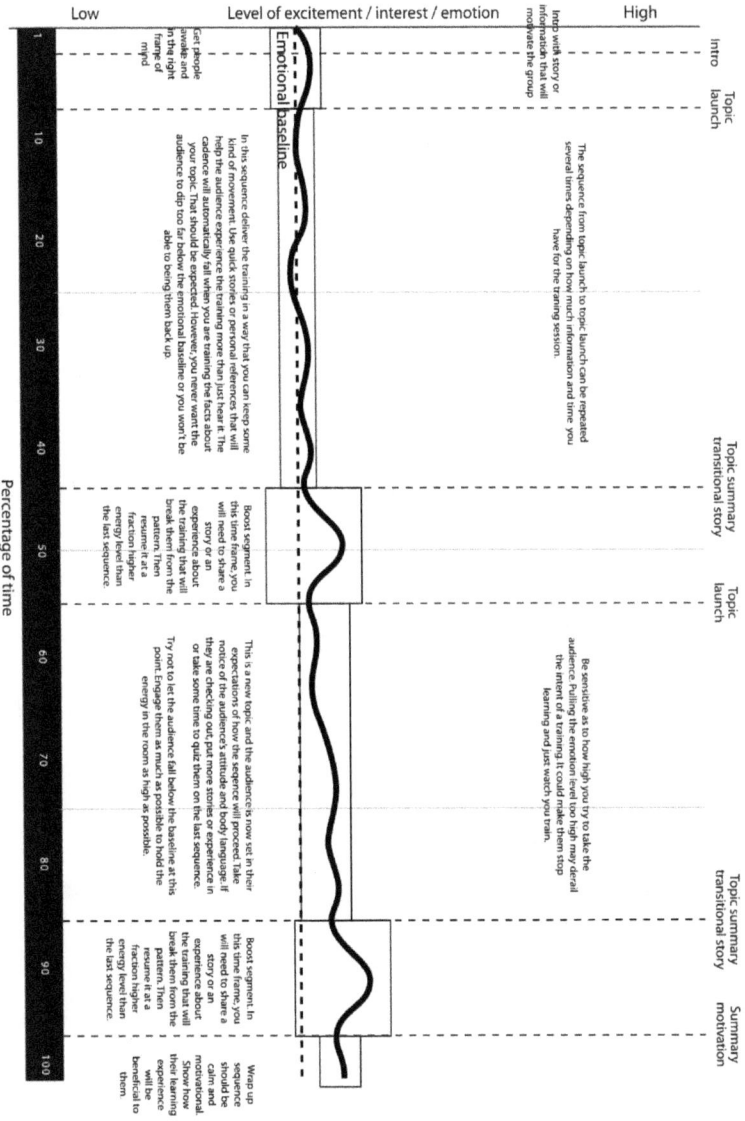

Intro with story or information that will motivate the group

Get people awake and in the right frame of mind

The sequence from topic launch to topic launch can be repeated several times depending on how much information and time you have for the training session.

In this sequence deliver the training in a way that you can keep some kind of movement. Use quick stories or personal references that will help the audience experience the training more than just hear it. The cadence will automatically fall when you are training the facts about your topic. That should be expected. However, you never want the audience to dip too far below the emotional baseline or you won't be able to bring them back up.

Boost segment. In this time frame, you will need to share a story or an experience about the training that will break them from the pattern. Then resume it at a fraction higher energy level than the last sequence.

Be sensitive as to how high you try to take the audience. Pulling the emotion level too high may derail the intent of a training. It could make them stop learning and just watch you train.

This is a new topic and the audience is now set in their expectations of how the sequence will proceed. Take notice of the audience's attitude and body language. If they are checking out, put more stories or experience in or take some time to quiz them on the last sequence. Try not to let the audience fall below the baseline at this point. Engage them as much as possible to hold the energy in the room as high as possible.

Boost segment. In this time frame, you will need to share a story or an experience about the training that will break them from the pattern. Then resume it at a fraction higher energy level than the last sequence.

Wrap up sequence should be calm and motivational. Show how their learning experience will be beneficial to them.

Grasp the subject, the words will follow.

- Cato The Elder

Chapter 5
Control

Knowing and Owning Your Content

Owning your content, or at least having rights to use it, is very important to your credibility. Using stock photography or quotes from others will add credibility and a level of professionalism to your presentation, as long as the audience isn't under the impression that you shot the photo or claim to have come up with a quote that they have already heard. Once you have the rights to a photograph or video, you don't always need to add a footnote on your slide crediting the source. However, if you are quoting statistics or an individual, you should put the source on the bottom right-hand corner of your slide. You don't always have to address the source, but often revealing the source adds credibility to the statement or statistic.

Beyond legally owning the rights to your material, psychologically taking ownership of your content will provide you with a level of passion that can't be faked. I was asked to speak to a grocery store chain that was holding a banquet for their local providers. These are small to medium-sized local companies that either grow or produce their own products within 100 miles of the stores. As I was preparing the presentation, I wondered how I would relate to this audience. I don't produce or grow a consumable product, and I don't raise chickens or cows. As I started planning my presentation, I realized that I did have one thing in common with most of these companies. I had started my own business; I was an entrepreneur. That was something that I owned, something that I knew a great deal about. When I shared a catastrophic experience in my business that actually caused me to permanently lose half of my hearing, I could see them turn to each other and nod their heads agreeing with me that being an entrepreneur is not for the faint of heart. They had all experienced stressful times building a business, and from that moment on, I was one of them. They believed that I honestly knew what I was talking about, even if it didn't relate to their business directly.

If someone asks a question that you actually don't know the answer to during your presentation, or if your presentation time allows for a question and answer period, be careful to retain your equity with the group. Never commit to something that you aren't sure of. I use phrases like, "I'm not sure about that, but this is what I think," or "That is a great question, and I'm not sure what the answer is, but I'm going to look into it. Thank you for asking." I am mortified when presenters finish their presentations and an audience member puts them on the spot and they try to fake their way through an answer. People are understanding if you are honest with them. Your opinion, on the other hand, is debatable, but you are entitled to it. Having an opinion demonstrates your passion on the subject and shows the audience that you are committed.

Tactics:

- Own what you put in your presentation— legally and emotionally.

- Research your audience and find some common ground.

- If you encounter something you actually don't know, don't fake it. Own the fact that you don't know, and inform your audience that you'll do some research.

- Strive for credibility in your presentation. Build trust with your audience to reach your objective.

Dealing with Hecklers

First, let's define heckler. Typically, a heckler is someone who shouts from the audience in an attempt to rattle the presenter. But sometimes a heckler doesn't even realize what they're doing. In 2013, one of our presenters was doing a presentation to a high school audience. He was presenting a program that we branded, "Don't Drive Stupid." It was a program that was designed to talk to high school students in their tone and language. Our presenter, Jeff, had just opened the presentation and was ramping the audience's emotions up his cadence line, when a teacher walked to the stage and stopped him. She said to him, "Do you realize that the phrase, 'Don't Drive Stupid' is grammatically incorrect?" That was an unintentional heckler. She completely derailed his presentation, and the entire audience wanted to know what she had said to him. Jeff simply said to her, "Wow, I'll let my boss know. Thanks?" He then addressed the audience and said, "How many of you have ever driven stupidly?" She nodded her head, signifying that he phrased that sentence correctly and sat down. Jeff was able to regain his momentum and finish the presentation. Getting into a discussion about the phrase would have destroyed his presentation.

It's very difficult to prepare for these kinds of interruptions. They come out of thin air and often have nothing to do with your objective. Sadly, these situations will always disrupt your cadence. You may not be able to stop the disruption, but you can choose how you mitigate it. Jeff could have said to the teacher, "Yes, we know, it's just supposed to be clever. It doesn't have to make sense. It's a brand statement, not a sentence," and on and on. But that would have only engaged her longer. It wouldn't have helped him recover his position and get the audience back under control. The best practice is to take the shortest route. This may mean saying something like, "Oh, thank you for bringing that to my attention. I'll work on that." Or Jeff's response, "I'll let my boss know." This comment let her know that he wasn't the person that created the phrase, and therefore there wasn't anything he could do about it. He disarmed her nicely and pulled the air out of her comment. Try to use a response that is disarming and won't drag you into further confrontation.

Some presenters use a ricochet approach. When someone interrupts them or actually heckles them from the audience, they fire off a rocket from the deck to shut them down. Usually, this is an insult of some kind that is intended to push the heckler back into their chair with enough shock that they don't try it again. This may work at times, but often it will cause the individual to amplify their efforts and could make the situation worse. You risk losing the entire audience with this approach. If this individual is respected by the audience, you may never regain their trust or your cadence. You just became the enemy.

A better alternative is to find a quick alignment with them or offer to talk with them afterward so you can bring the situation to a close as quickly as possible. If a member of the audience interrupts you, even though you didn't invite the audience to engage, and you address the comment openly, you risk turning your presentation into a question and answer session. When this happens, you are no longer presenting because you have lost control of the cadence. Your planned objective is no longer your target. You are now a firefighter working to put out fires and keep things under control.

Tactics:

- Find the quickest comment to bring the heckler under control, even if it means agreeing with them.

- Invite them to meet with you following the presentation where you can discuss their comment.

- Try not to engage them. This will only draw out the interruption and disconnect you from the rest of the audience.

- Keep questions under control so your presentation doesn't turn into a Q&A session.

Regaining Your Cadence

In the event you lose control of your cadence by responding to an audience member or spending too much time on a tangent, regroup your thoughts and move your body position before you speak. Pause. Taking a few seconds as you physically move will bring the audience's attention together. Getting your thoughts aligned before you begin will help you decide if you need to inject a story, or if you are close enough to a transition point that you can get back on track and continue. I have used comments like, "That is a very interesting point, we should look into that later," or "I appreciate your input. As I was saying . . . ." These are disarming comments that acknowledge their comment or statement, but they allow you to realign the presentation and regain your momentum. If you are giving a presentation and you expect a lot of interruptions, you could bring in a paper board or use a white board to write the comments down. By writing them down you can express that you'll get to them later, if possible. After you have written it on the board, resume speaking before you turn back to the audience. This may help deter others from making comments that will keep you off your cadence.

If you have a specific person who is creating contention during your presentation, simply move your body away from them and don't look in their direction. Believe me, the people around them will understand why you're avoiding their section of the audience. If you don't reward their behavior, they may just give up. If they continue, most likely they will have to elevate their comments to a point that the audience members around them may try to shut them down.

Losing track of your cadence isn't a catastrophe, but it does cause some fragmentation in your audience. Dipping too low or exploding too high can cause you to overcorrect. Be careful not to make erratic jumps in your presentation. They are often misunderstood and can confuse the audience.

As a member of the National Speakers Association, we usually hold our chapter meetings at a medical training facility in Salt Lake. It is a beautiful venue and the rooms are great and adaptable for our large group. At our monthly meetings we usually have a special guest speaker come in and present to our group. During every presentation, the hospital PA system announces a code alert. This code is initiated with three or four loud tones and is followed by a code statement calling on specific medical staff to an emergency or event. I am always interested to see how our guest presenters handle the interruption. These are professional speakers that are very nimble on their feet. Usually, they wait until the code ends, and when they draw in a breath to comment about it, the code happens again. Yes, it always happens twice. I get a kick out of watching them recover. Some make a joke about it and ask if we all need to leave the room. Others have just paused, and when the code ended, they picked up right where they left off. I personally feel that those who just try to ignore the event miss an opportunity to bond with the group. Those who make a joke or comment quickly defuse the situation and adjust their cadence momentarily to lift the group back up to where they were before the interruption.

Interruptions will happen. It may be an AV issue or some other kind of disturbance. Just take a deep breath, and make a light-hearted comment about it, smile, and move on.

Tactics:

- Prepare a few comments that help you acknowledge and close distractions.

- In smaller groups, use a paper board or white board to write comments down and move on.

- In the event you get far off your topic, stop the presentation and restate your objective. This will help the audience refocus.

- A relevant story can bridge the gap and will always help get your cadence back on track.

Dealing with Personal Tics and Tendencies

I have been working in the communications industry my entire adult life. My children have been exposed to the advertising and marketing industry at the dinner table nightly. Twenty-five years ago, I was sitting in church with them, and following a talk given by one of our neighbors, my eldest son turned to me and said, "Dad, he said 'um' thirty-five times in a ten-minute talk. That's bad, isn't it?" What have I done? Have I turned my own children into critical judges of people's presentation skills? Over the years all four of them have expressed to me that their experience growing up in the wake of my career in presentations has had a profound impact in their lives.

What my son was talking about is a verbal tic. The terms "um", "uh", "so", and "like" are verbal tics that usually sneak out when a person is trying to speak without having first practiced their presentation. In an attempt to sound loose, they try to just wing their way through an outline of thoughts. These tics or crutches appear when they are processing what to say next.

Spending some extra time phrasing or just practicing the presentation will help eliminate them. If you're not sure if you have them or not, simply record yourself during your next presentation, and then listen to it. If you have tics, you'll hear them. It will take some practice to eliminate them, but your impact as a presenter will be much stronger and it will be well worth the effort.

Physical tics are equally as distracting. Physical tics are typically habits or a product of being nervous. I have often worked with presenters that say, "I just don't know what to do with my hands. They always feel like they are in my way."

In the fall of 2000, I was working with a senior manager at one of the world's largest banks, helping her get ready to present to her clients in their treasury division. When we designed her presentation I instructed our creative team to remove the bullets and most of the words on her slides. I assumed the deck she sent us was her notes on the slides to give us clear instructions for what to design. Much to my surprise, when we met for the first time to go over her deck, she panicked because none of her words were on her slides. I assured her that she would do fine and there was just too much content on the slides for her to present.

As she began practicing her presentation, I noticed something astonishing. She held her right hand directly under her chin, at the center of her chest, palm up. At first, I thought that she would drop it as she got more comfortable, but she never did. She did the whole presentation with her arm and hand in that position. I told her to try to move the remote to her right hand this time and see how that felt. It was unbelievable. She positioned her left arm and hand in the exact same position. I stopped her in the middle of her presentation and asked her if she realized it and she said, "No, I didn't. Let me try again."

She found that day that she had a physical tic that was distracting. The more she tried to stop it, the worse it got. I tried everything to help her: with a remote, without a remote, with a glass in her right hand and the remote in her left, which helped a little bit because now she held a glass directly in front of her instead of an open palm.

After several hours of working with her, she told me that she thought it was because she was nervous about presenting the new slides. She felt that removing her content from the slides might actually be the problem. She had practiced the presentation the way she sent it to me and we decided to try going through her original presentation deck.

She still had the tic, but I don't think she realized it because she turned and faced the screen the whole time.

She ended up presenting with the glass in her hand that conference and began the process of overcoming a tic that was incredibly distracting. It took several presentations, but she overcame it and became far more confident presenting.

So, how do you figure out if you have a physical tic? It is very simple. At your next presentation or even when you're practicing, video tape yourself. When you play it back, look for patterns or repetitive motions that you make that seem distracting. Do you move at all? Do you do a three-step move? Do you hold your arms awkwardly? Do you throw them around wildly? Do you keep one in your pocket or hold them in the same position over and over again? If you don't notice them, then they might not be too bad. If you want to take a closer look, you can play the video in fast forward, which will amplify them if you have any.

Don't be discouraged if you find something. Most people have some kind of nervous tic that happens when they present. Identifying them and committing to practice them away is the key to overcoming them.

Tactics:

- Listen to a recording of your presentation to identify if you have any verbal tics.

- Practice phrasing your presentation more if you find that you struggle with them. The more comfortable you are with your presentation, the less you'll use them.

- Identify physical tics by videotaping yourself and watching it objectively.

- Play the video in fast forward to amplify any tics you might have.

- Practice overcoming them. If you don't, you'll use them more. Remember, we perfect what we practice.

The success of your presentation will be judged not by the knowledge you send, but by what the listener receives.

- Lily Walters

Chapter 6
Connection

Relatability and Connection

I briefly mentioned this previously, but let me expound on the notion. Everyone was once 7-years-old. We have all heard the term "inner child," but I focus specifically on 7-year-olds because this is the age that I remember things starting to make sense. Before that, if it tasted like sugar, I ate it. If my mom said it was right, I did it. At the age of seven, I started hearing that little Mike voice in my head that said things like, "Hmm, do I like that or not?" or "That doesn't seem right," or "Does that mean they don't like me or they do like me?" Feelings and emotions become a major part of our lives at about 7-years-old. How we feel starts to play a much bigger part in our decision-making process. Having raised four kids, I experienced this as a parent, and yes, everyone is a bit different, but feelings enter the equation in everyone's decision-making process nonetheless.

According to Forbes Magazine, a message delivered as a story can be recalled up to 22 times more often than just the facts alone. Also, Media.net reported that emotions drive 80% of the choices we make every day, while practicality and objectivity only represent about 20% of our decision-making. In fact, in an article on Buffer.com titled, "What Listening to a Story Does to Our Brains," they claim that stories activate seven parts of the human brain. They cause the listener to experience neural coupling, which means they make the story their own. Dopamine is released and causes an increase in emotion, and the cortex is stimulated, causing both sides of the brain to react. In other words, stories activate our imagination, senses, and bodies.

When giving a presentation, if you take into consideration the inner child in your audience members, you will find it much easier to relate to them. This doesn't mean that you talk down to them or treat them any differently; it just means that you strive to deliver your information with some emotional connection. After all, a presentation void of emotion is really just a report or a documentary. Connecting with your audience is what generates their perceived value in your message and validates that it was a good use of their time.

It's interesting to think that as you present, the people in the room are all there with a relatively common interest or expectation. If you were to interview each one of them individually, you would find a wide range of hobbies, tastes, and opinions. You would also probably find some similarities or commonalities that bring them together. Learning how to communicate and connect with their common inner child can be a powerful tool to engage their emotions in support of your objectives.

Tactics:

- Look for ways to engage your audience's emotions.

- For relatability, try connecting with their inner child.

- Negative emotions are hard to overcome. Plan your information carefully to protect your audience from getting upset beyond your ability to recover.

Conduct Instant Research

Sometimes when you are giving a presentation, you make assumptions that everyone is tracking right along. You interpret their body language and do everything right to move your cadence based on your perception of the audiences input. Early on in my career, just as desktop publishing entered our world, I attended an Aldus Training Camp in Southern California. Aldus *(later purchased by Adobe)* produced software that was created to help designers put together page layouts, design graphics, produce presentations and other disciplines in the graphic arts world. I was an Apple consultant at the time, and I was training companies on how to do desktop publishing in their own offices. While attending the training, I kept saying to myself, "Oh man, I could totally do this." I did a little math to figure out how much money they made doing the event and decided, I was going for it. I came home and spent several months developing a workshop/seminar all about desktop publishing. The only difference was that I was determined to give my attendees even more. I wouldn't just focus on the Aldus software, but I would work through the entire process, starting with what equipment to buy to get started and ending with a printed, finished product. This workshop,

I believed, was going to be the most amazing and comprehensive workshop ever.

I created a three-inch binder of information and samples that I called, "The Learning Curve." Oh yeah, this was going to blow people's mind. I set up three shows along the Wasatch Front in Utah. The first show was in Ogden, and I had about 20 people show up. I was charging $750 per person, and back in those days, that was a lot of money for someone to shell out. I had paid $950 for the one I attended in California, so I figured this was a great deal. I started the show by going over the equipment that people needed to have or purchase in order to do desktop publishing. It took about two hours to cover everything from the monitor to scanners to external data storage. We took a break, and after some refreshments and quiet conversations they came back to their seats. It was relatively quiet, so I figured they were ready to go. I started up the training again, teaching them how to scan in an image. During this demonstration, I looked out at the audience, and they were all just sitting there, staring at me. That body language said to me that I was boring them to death. Nobody was taking notes or anything. So, I adjusted my cadence and threw some gas on the fire—so to speak.

I was exhausted after the first day because I had covered so much ground, and I didn't think I could go any faster. At the close of the first day, they gave me a round of applause and left. The next morning, only 16 of the 20 returned to finish the workshop. That was crazy to me because they had paid for the two days, and I wasn't too thrilled about the idea of giving them a refund. I had a great night's rest and was ready to give this group of 16 even more. By the end of the second day, the audience wandered out, and I felt like a total failure. I had absolutely let them down. I told my wife that I really didn't know what else to add to make it more valuable for the next group coming in only four days. I knew it was so much better than the other workshops that I had attended on the topic. I just couldn't figure out what was happening. Was it me?

With the help of my wife, I picked myself up and dusted myself off and recommitted to the next audience. After the first break in the morning of the first day of the workshop, the audience of 45 people was acting the exact same way. I felt like I had lost their attention completely.

Then, an older gentleman by the name of Nick came up to me and said, "Wow, I have never seen anything like that. I can't believe how good you are at this and how much you know. How did you learn it all?" I told him that I had been an Apple consultant for a few years and had done a lot of desktop publishing. Nick was the only one in the group who came up to me. The others were just like the previous group, all talking quietly at the back of the room in small groups. I asked Nick what he liked the most so far, and he said, "Oh, I have no idea what you're talking about, you lost me at the word scanner." I just stared at him, "What do you mean, Nick?" He said, "I don't think anyone in here has any idea what you're talking about, but it is amazing to watch you go over it all. I am afraid that I'll never be able to do desktop publishing. It's just way too deep for me."

You can't imagine how I felt. I brought the group back together and asked them. "Okay, before we get going again, I just want to ask you all if I am going too fast or too slow?" I waited until someone said, "I'm embarrassed to say this, but I think I am in the wrong workshop; this is way too advanced for me." Everyone in the room agreed with her and started to laugh. So I asked them, "What would you like me to cover again; I want you all to get something out of this. I know you paid good money for it, and I want it to be worth it to you." I never finished going over the equipment section. I didn't even show them how to scan in an image. I literally covered 5% of my material.

In the next show, with 35 people in attendance I started it with this comment, "I will be stopping throughout this workshop to make sure you are comfortable with what I have taught you. If you are lost or confused, please let me know, and I'll cover it again." I covered about the same amount of information, and the group gave me a standing ovation at the end.

Four companies that were in attendance hired me on contract to help develop their desktop publishing departments. Nick was my first client. I worked with his company for three years, and in those three years, I still didn't cover everything that was in the Learning Curve workshop.

Throughout your presentation, it's so important to ascertain if your audience is tracking with you. And as you can see from my previous example, you can easily misread their body language. It's a sound practice to plan specific points in your cadence to conduct some research. Ask your audience if they are comfortable. Do they need any clarifications or explanations? Their body language will tell you a lot. If you make a comment about something, and you throw into your comment a response hook, you should get some kind of reaction from some of the audience. This is how a response hook works: "That is how you scan in an image to your computer. Does that make sense?" Then pay attention to your audience. They probably won't respond out loud, but you are bound to have a few nodders that you have identified throughout your presentation. If they don't nod, bluntly ask the audience if you need to cover the topic again or answer any questions. This technique holds true outside of the workshop setting. Don't assume your audience is tracking with you. If you question it, ask them.

Having been partially deaf for several years, I have learned how to read and interpret body language pretty well. Reading body language is a very powerful skill. However, it can be very difficult to decipher the difference between, "Hmm, that is very interesting," and "Yikes, I hope I am not the only one who is totally and utterly lost."

Tactics:

- Read your audience's body language, but take the time to clarify it.

- Make sure you are delivering your message at your audience's desired speed.

- If you aren't sure if your audience is tracking with you, ASK THEM.

Visualize the Whole Presentation

I'm sure you're familiar with the idiom, "You can't see the forest for the trees." Sometimes when you are getting ready to make a presentation, you can find yourself so focused on your content that you lose track of your objective. There are multiple ways to ensure that you are not too "deep in the forest." A Cadence Chart will help you visualize your whole presentation at a glance. If you are using PowerPoint or Keynote software, you can also view all your slides in a tiled view. I find it very helpful to create parent/child slide groups for my visuals. This allows you to tuck slides under a transition or a key parent slide. In these software packages, you can minimize the child slides and view only the parent slides. This helps you see the sections, or keyframes, of your presentation without the extra visuals. This will also help you open just sections of your presentation and work on them independently.

By viewing all of your key parent slides, you should be able to get a feel for your whole presentation. This exercise will also help you visualize if you are overworking or under-working a topic. Remember, you are looking for balance and cohesion for your presentation. If you can't visualize the cadence in this exercise, you might want to adjust your content to lock it in.

Psychologically, this will help you envision yourself giving the presentation in a mental image—similar to how a downhill ski racer closes their eyes and feels their upcoming race. If you've ever watched them get ready, you can see them moving their heads, shoulders, and arms as they mentally race the course. They race the course perfectly in their mind's eye. When the starting gate opens, their race is practically muscle memory. They are going at incredibly high speeds and their body is reacting just how their brain practiced it.

Tactics:

- Use a Cadence Chart to visualize the entire presentation.

- Visualizing your whole presentation in a mental image will help you to know when you need to adjust your cadence.

- Envision yourself actually giving the presentation in your mind before you actually present it.

Who or What is the Competition?

Some of the people I have worked with tell me that they feel like they are defending themselves when they make a presentation. Sometimes that might be true if you are, in fact, defending a position. I think this feeling often arises most during a sales presentation. But just because you are trying to win some business doesn't mean your audience is the competition. In fact, they are actually looking for someone to become their partner in most cases. In this situation, they are not the competition. The other vendors trying to win their business are your competition. When this happens, try to remember that as far as your audience is concerned, you are on the same team. They are holding tryouts. Your objective is to present them with a product or solution that helps them win more business or become better. If you work on creating a perception with them that your offering is superior to your competition, and you are vested in their success, your chances of winning the business are much better. If you are always in defense mode, they'll probably feel that friction and they will not be comfortable. Connecting with your audience in every situation is the key to engaging their emotions. That connection is the psychological glue that connects your information with their feelings. Believe it or not, everyone you present to goes through a process, consciously or subconsciously, to decide whether they like you or not.

In situations where your audience is, in fact, the competition or opponent, your ability to connect with them may be difficult but is still very important. They might automatically have the preconceived opinion that they don't like you. One of your objectives should be to overcome this initial perception. You should at least try to level that opinion so their emotions about you or your company don't overpower your objective.

In 2007, the director of the Utah Department of Transportation was tasked with reporting to the engineering and construction industry that federal and state funding had been cut, and there would be fewer projects happening in the coming years. Going into the presentation, the director knew he was going to get hammered by the audience. They were very in tune with the industry and knew that there were some hard issues coming their way. It wasn't his fault, but he was the one who had to deliver the news. We worked on his presentation and cadence to strategically soften the audience's emotions before he broke the news. At the beginning of his presentation, he showed images of some of the amazing work that many of them had accomplished over the years and assured them that their contribution to the state was both amazing and well-respected, locally and nationally. As he broke the news about the budget cuts, he explained that it meant that everyone, including his department, was going to have to be more innovative and creative. Everyone was going to have to do more with less. He then showed some of the recent projects where new techniques and innovations had been implemented and assured them that as they all worked through this tough time, things were going to get better. As resources became available, they would continue to lead the nation with the most innovative, effective, and efficient transportation system.

With this cadence strategy, he was able to mitigate their emotions and deliver the bad news without any repercussions. In fact, the first question from the audience was a compliment to him for being honest and forthright with them and thanking him for representing their industry with such class and professionalism. He was able to control the situation and connect with them as an endeared advocate.

As you prepare your presentation strategy, identify your opponent. Is it the topic, the audience (their background or their opinion), another company? Or, is there even a real competitor? Just because you're presenting, doesn't mean that something is competing with you. If you feel this way when you present, you need to work though it because your audience will feel that tension, and it will make it more difficult for you to connect with them.

Tactics:

• Overcome feelings of competition by identifying any possible opponent and addressing your strategy to win them over.

• When you are presenting to an opponent, strategically plan to mitigate any initial emotions and create a cadence that will get you to your objective.

- Visualize the audience as your friends. Go into the presentation with good vibes and high expectations.

- Do your research before your presentation to identify any potential opponents, whether they are topics or people.

Humor and Stories

Many techniques will help you connect with your audience. Your topic, experience, background, even your presentation style will be part of your impact. But very few techniques will help you connect with your audience faster, deeper, and stronger than your sense of humor and your storytelling ability. Not everyone has a sense of humor. Well, let's say not everyone has a *great* sense of humor.

It's so interesting during the first moments of your presentation to see who in the audience has a good sense of humor and who doesn't. I always like starting off with something that gets the audience aligned with me and in a light-hearted mood. It helps me identify the hot spots in the audience and helps me gauge if I am connecting with them or not.

When you're injecting your sense of humor, make sure you project your voice. Sometimes when we toss out a funny line or statement, we lower our voice as part of the delivery. That works well when it's only a few people in a private conversation. But, if you are talking to a larger group or using a microphone, they may miss the line completely, and your attempt could fail. Use your body language and your movement to emphasize the statement if possible.

I have found it very helpful to watch stand-up comedians as often as I can. Not just because I love comedians, but because I am fascinated by how they perfect their timing and physical movements in their show. I am not suggesting that you become a comedian, but these people work very hard on their delivery to get to their audience's sense of humor and have usually perfected the art of connecting with their audience.

This may sound harsh, but if you don't think you have a sense of humor, it's okay. Just be sensitive to the fact that trying to be funny, if you just organically are not funny, could feel... clunky.

In the spring of 2019, I was presenting to a large group and the meeting planner neglected to ask me for a bio prior to their event. The vice president, came over to me in a panic with a pad of paper and started asking me questions to build one on the spot. I just smiled and gave her a few things, including a couple of things that I thought would be funny, "I am working on becoming a golf pro, an extreme back country mountain ski guide, and a Jedi Knight." She wrote it down and thought that the group would find it funny when their president introduced me. I don't think he read the bio she gave him until he was standing at the mic. He literally read it verbatim, and when he got to the funny part, he didn't change tempo, volume, or tone. The vice president and I were the only two who laughed.

As I started my presentation, I could see some of the audience had a confused look on their faces and were whispering to each other, so I felt like I had to clear the air about my hobbies and aspirations of becoming a Jedi Knight. Still no laughter because they weren't sure that was what they heard anyway. I literally had to just apologize for trying to be funny, and it was only then that I got some laughter.

Laughter is a strong emotional reaction. If your topic allows for humor, plan opportunities to get your audience to laugh.

Aside from the obvious benefits as a presenter of relieving some of your tension. Laughter will help your audience feel more comfortable and help them become more open and receptive to your message.

The Mayo Clinic Stress Team published on their website *(www.mayoclinic.org)* the following about the short-term and long-term impacts of humor. I think the science of the impact of laughter is fascinating and will impact your storytelling.

A good laugh has many great short-term effects. When you start to laugh, it doesn't just lighten your load mentally, it actually induces physical changes in your body.

Laughter enhances your intake of oxygen-rich air, stimulates your heart, lungs and muscles, and increases the endorphins that are released by your brain. A rollicking laugh fires up and then cools down your stress response, and it can increase and then decrease your heart rate and blood pressure.

Laughter isn't just a quick pick-me-up, though. It's also good for you over the long-term. Negative thoughts manifest into chemical reactions that can affect your body by bringing more stress into your system.

In summary, using humor is a great way to lighten the atmosphere in your presentation and set the mood of your audience to a calm and receptive attitude. I am not proposing that you turn your presentation into a stand-up routine but that you consider using humor as a connection tool with your audience.

Storytelling is the most powerful tool to engage the emotion of your audience. I am always surprised when I hear people tell me that they don't have any stories. How could you possibly exist in today's world without a lot of stories?

If you feel that you are one of the people that don't think they have stories, take a minute and open your photo app on your phone. As you swipe through your photos, you'll see images that relate to events that are stories. Maybe not every photo, but there will be some that are connected to a series of events that lead to a story.

Some people are gifted storytellers, others have to work at it. Being able to identify your stories is a great start. My method is simple. To begin the process you have to only look for one thing - a climax. Something that is out of the ordinary and had an impact on your life. Then, find what that story taught you, the lesson. Now, you are on your way.

The Story Cadence Chart

Storytelling is skill that can be developed with some basic structural planning and practice. In 1863, Gustav Freytag, a German playwright and novelist, developed a diagram called the Freytag Pyramid. It is a dramatic structure outlining seven key steps in successful storytelling: exposition, inciting incident, rising action, climax, falling action, resolution, and denouement. Over my years of studying storytelling, I have found that most stories don't actually happen in this pattern but they can usually be retold in the pattern. After years of developing stories, I have modified the pattern for presentations and created a Story Cadence Chart that works for short stories used in presentations almost every time.

I use two tools to formulate and develop my stories:

Story Grid—the Story Grid *(shown here)* is a simple spreadsheet. You can use Microsoft Excel, Apple Numbers or Google Sheets to create it. It will need to have columns to enable you to capture the basic components of your stories. In order to provide more detail for my stories, I capture three rising action

Date	Exposition	Inciting Incident	Rising Action	Rising Action	Rising Action	Climax	Falling Action	Falling Action	Resolution	Lesson
Sept. 1978	Home from school watching Gilligan's Island in the basement	Dad came home during the day. Thought I might be in trouble.	Got in the Dodge D-100 Ranger. Told me it was his Nephew's Sales. Did the story	"Tell me about Bigfoot", talking	Pulling into the driveway. Dad bangs on the dash and screams	Dad jumps off the seat between the buckets onto the hood of the truck	Spends the evening teaching me room's consoling Mom and I	In the morning Dad is reading the paper and asks if I learned anything	"Yes Dad, you saw him to didn't you?"	Storytelling

events and two falling action events. These help me to remember key moments that are important to develop the story later. I also include a lesson column at the end to provide me with a column that I can sort my stories with. It really helps to organize them by the experience I learned from the story, and it makes it easy to find stories that will fit the topic and audience in every presentation.

The column titles are: **Date, Exposition, Inciting Incident, Rising Action, Rising Action, Rising Action, Climax, Falling Action, Falling Action, Resolution, and Lesson.**

Story Cadence Tool—Using my original Cadence Charting System, I have created an Apple Keynote and Microsoft PowerPoint file as a tool to help create Story Cadence Charts. We offer these tools to companies that complete our Presenter Evolution workshop. This tool helps attendees organize their elements from their Story Grid into a Cadence Chart. The pattern for a story is relatively constant for presentations. They should follow the pattern shown here to be concise, while achieving the objective for the audience. Obviously, you can always create a Story Cadence Chart manually. My tool was used to develop the Story Cadence Chart seen here as well as the Cadence Charts in this book.

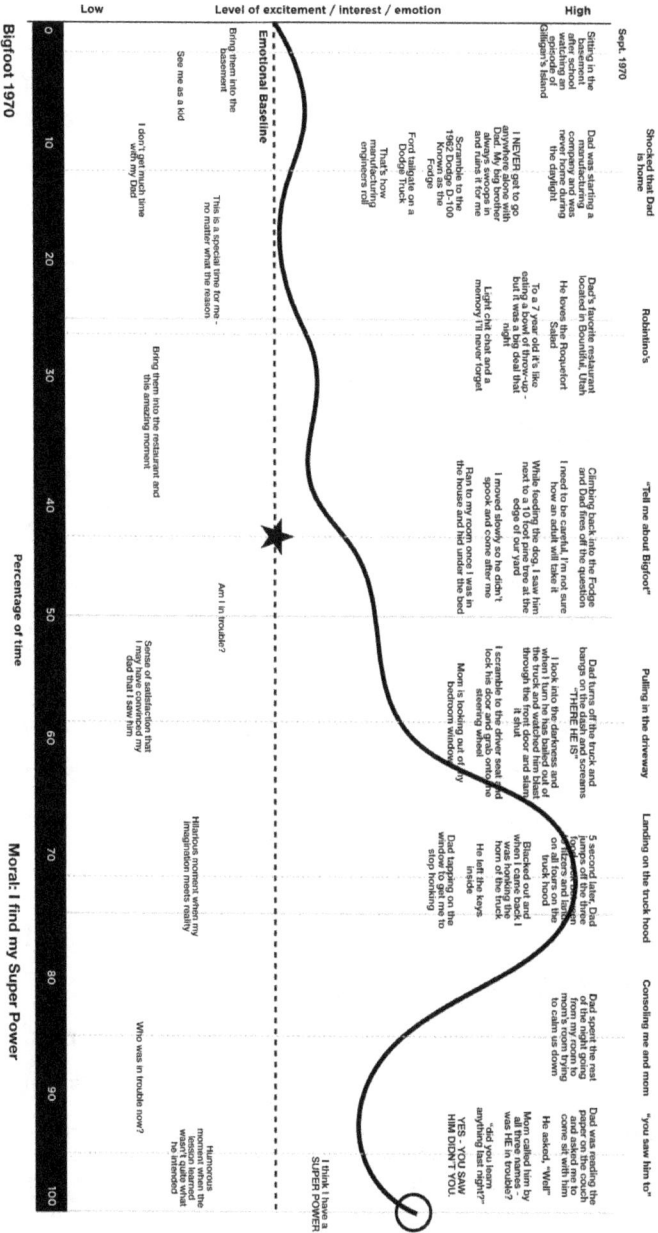

Low | Level of excitement / interest / emotion | High

Bigfoot 1970

Sept. 1970

Emotional Baseline

Percentage of time

Moral: I find my Super Power

0   10   20   30   40   50   60   70   80   90   100

Shocked that Dad is home

Sitting in the basement after school watching an episode of Gilligan's Island

Dad was starting a manufacturing company and was never home during the daylight

I NEVER get to go anywhere alone with Dad. My big brother always swoops in and ruins it for me

Scramble to the 1982 Dodge D-100 Known as the Fodge

Ford tailgate on a Dodge Truck

Bring them into the basement

This is a special time for me - no matter what the reason

See me as a kid

I don't get much time with my Dad

Robitino's

Dad's favorite restaurant located in Bountiful, Utah

He loves the Roquefort Salad

To a 7 year old it's like eating a bowl of throw-up - but it was a big deal that night

Light chit chat and a memory I'll never forget

Bring them into the restaurant and this amazing moment

"Tell me about Bigfoot"

Climbing back into the Fodge and Dad fires off the question

I need to be careful, I'm not sure how an adult will take it

While feeding the dog I saw him next to a 10 foot pine tree at the edge of our yard

I moved slowly so he didn't spook and come after me

Ran to my room once I was in the house and hid under the bed

★

Am I in trouble?

Pulling in the driveway

Dad turns off the truck and bangs on the dash and screams "THERE HE IS"

I look into the darkness and when I turn he has bailed out of the truck and walked out through the front door and slung it shut

I scramble to the driver seat and when I came back I lock his door and grab onto the steering wheel

Mom is looking out of my bedroom window

Sense of satisfaction that I may have convinced my dad that I saw him

Landing on the truck hood

5 second later, Dad jumps off the three foot cement fountain and lands on all fours on the truck hood

Blacked out and when I came back I was honking the horn of the truck

He left the keys inside

Dad tapping on the window to get me to stop honking

Hilarious moment when my imagination meets reality

Who was in trouble now?

Consoling me and mom

Dad spent the rest of the night going from my room to mom's room trying to calm us down

He asked, "Well"

Mom called him by all three names - "did you learn anything last night?"

Dad was reading the paper on the couch and asked me to come sit with him

"you saw him to"

YES - YOU SAW HIM DIDN'T YOU.

I think I have a SUPER POWER

Humorous moment when the lesson learned wasn't quite what he intended

You can practice this by taking a memorable event in your life and laying the elements onto this framework to create an impactful story, a story that has the ability to impact the audience with whom it relates. Telling a story that isn't relevant or interesting to a group will not generate the emotional connection you may be looking for.

I have always been a storyteller; in fact, my mother used to warned me that I needed to be careful about telling a story better than the event actually was. As a child, I never understood that. Why wouldn't I want to make it better if I had time to think about it again? And by better, I mean more engaging. Her concern was that the more I told the stories, the more the specifics were blurred into fiction. Bluntly said, I think she was afraid that I was adding things that didn't actually happen. To my mothers great relief, I have been able to separate actual events from things that are in my imagination—without ruining the story.

When I was 14 years old, my family experienced a terrible accident. My father was helping my oldest sister put shingles on her new home. It was October 29th, my mother's 44th birthday, and she had just arrived at my sister's house. Suddenly, a gust of wind blew a few bundles of shingles that had been balanced on the peak of the roof down the west side of the home. My father was working on that side and was at the edge of the roof. As the packages came sliding down towards him, he tried to quickly jump over them but ended up stepping on the last couple of packages, which caused him to fall. In desperation, he turned around and tried to jump to a cherry tree that was just beyond the home, but the tree branches just spun him upside down, and he fell two stories to the ground. Badly injured and unable to move, he laid motionless on the ground. We were all in shock and extremely traumatized. I was sent to the road to wait for the ambulance. My mind was racing as to why it was taking them so long and why this would happen to my dad. It seemed like it took the ambulance forever to get there, but soon my father was taken to the hospital in critical condition. He passed away two days later from fatal brain trauma. Now, I know this is a tragic story, and just the facts are hard to read. But what happened to me in the years following this accident is insightful as it pertains to storytelling.

When I went back to junior high school, no one knew what to say to me. It had been weeks since the accident, but everyone knew what had happened. I would walk around the school alone, and even my closest friends would avoid talking to me because they had no idea how to approach me or what to say. In one of my classes, I put my head down and the teacher let me sleep through three periods. I woke up to a room full of kids that I didn't even know in a puddle of slobber. At this point, I felt like I was never going to get over losing my dad. Eventually, a girl my age came up to me as I sat on the bench by the front office, and she started to sob. "Mike, we are so sorry and none of us know what to say, but we love you." I just turned to her and said, "Cathy, I didn't die. I need all of you now more than ever." The next day all of my friends just embraced me, and it made a world of difference as I worked through the grieving process.

As the years went by, the fact that my father had passed away faded away to most of them. Their storybook lives seemed to carry on, while mine was being completely rewritten every day—without a father. I often thought to myself, "Nobody knows how I feel or how hard it is without my dad." I subconsciously started to use the tragedy to get their sympathy and attention. I perfected the story, not just the event, but the story of the event. Every time I told the story, the entire group would break down into tears. Somehow, I felt their emotions filled a void in my heart and helped them to better understand and connect with me. I had mastered the timing of when to stop talking and when to look down at the ground. I knew exactly when they were going to start to cry, and I would let them feel just a little bit of how I felt inside. As you can imagine, this isn't the healthiest pastime for a young teenage boy. One night, I was telling the story to a group of girls at a church activity, and right at the end of the story one of them said, "Well, that is really sad, but I am sure your father would want you to stop reliving it and move on with your life." The audible gasp of the other girls was shocking. They were so upset that she would say something like that. However, that young girl changed my life. She was the first person that I felt actually understood what I was doing and made me aware of it. Incidentally, that young girl grew up into an amazing woman, and I married her. She is my sweetheart, Ann.

That experience, and my experience in theater as a young man, helped me realize the power of storytelling. While I was at a National Speakers Association Chapter meeting one evening, I was sitting with two amazing ladies who were pursuing careers in the speaking industry. I told them how a story Cadence Chart works, and they asked me if I could show them. As an example, I relayed the facts about my father's accident and subsequent death using my Cadence

Chart and they said, "Oh, my gosh, did that really happen?" I said, "Yes, but now let me tell it in a story format. Prepare yourself—you're probably going to cry." I actually said that so they would be ready. Not even halfway through the story, before I had even told them that it was my mother's birthday, they both broke into tears and asked me to stop.

Learning how to cultivate your experiences into a story structure will help you bring emotion to your presentation. Emotions help us *connect* and relate to each other. Be very careful with people's emotions—they are not to be tampered with. Your objective is to connect with your audience through emotion, not manipulate them. You can actually upset an audience by sending one or more of them into an emotional overload. Some of the greatest speakers today have mastered the skill of capturing and connecting with their audience's emotions. Dan Clark, Tony Robbins, Rachel Hollis, and others have perfected the art of storytelling. The emotional connections they create quickly endear them, and their topics, to their audience. This connection is incredibly powerful.

Stories are the natural way you light up a person's imagination. You may want to have a visual that sets the tone of your story, but I wouldn't put images or animations on the screen behind you unless you produce the story into a video that virtually takes over for a time. If you are speaking, you should leverage your facial expressions, body movements, and the audience's imagination to paint the event's scenery. They will do a much better job creating the scenery and imagery in their minds than you can on a screen because they will draw upon their own experiences to create it. In essence, they will own your story, and it will mean so much more to them if they do.

Tactics:

- Practice the storytelling model on events in your life and write them down.

- Make sure your stories are relevant to the audience.

- Practice telling your stories independently to friends and family. See how they resonate with them.

- Use stories strategically. Too many random stories will confuse the audience.

- Leverage your body, voice, and the audience's imagination to paint the scenery for your story.

- Connect with your audience through emotion.

The ability to present is a Superpower, and the person that recognizes and develops it will generate more personal and professional value than by any other skill.

-Michael D. Brian

Chapter 7
Conclusion

Be One of the Few

To bring this book to a conclusion, my hope is that you will be able to add to your skillset as a presenter and join the select few who not only love to present but are actually very good at it. It's so interesting to me that when I ask groups that participate in our workshops if any of them love to present, many of them raise their hands. I think a lot of them believe that it is a prerequisite for leadership. When we do their filming and personal feedback sessions, I am always amazed by how many of them think they are great at it, but in reality they have a lot of room for improvement. Often, when we are discussing what they can do to get better, I hear this comment: "Every time I present, when I ask people what they thought about it afterward they always say that I was amazing." I just smile at them and say, "Did you expect any of them to say, 'Well, about that . . . you're okay, but you say 'um' and 'like' at the end of every sentence, and it was pretty hard to follow. Also, you looked at your slides the whole time so I couldn't really hear what you were saying." No, I doubt it. This is one of those social norms where people are not invested enough or too nervous of your reaction to really help you. Besides, they would most likely prefer that you did the presenting anyway, even if it is sub-par. The spotlight seems to burn a lot of people.

If you think of your own experiences attending presentations at work, or even paid presentations, how many of them do you come out of thinking, "Wow, that was really great, and it made a difference in my work or life."

Being able to present is usually an assumed prerequisite for people moving into management. If you look at most leaders in business, very few of them got their job because they were killer presenters. Sure, it may have played a role in their promotion, but can you imagine hearing someone say, "Yeah, that's our CEO. She never really accomplished much in her profession, but wow, she's a great presenter." Most people are promoted because they are amazing at their jobs or trained skillset. Management promotes them to lead others in that discipline in hopes of inspiring others to get better by their example. Sadly, this often means that the productivity or specialty the new leader provided to the company is now being pushed to the back of their responsibilities as they manage others. Being a manager means that you are shepherding people. You are responsible for making sure that they are progressing and productive for the company.

I have heard so many people say that they hear in employee reviews and surveys that, "Management doesn't communicate well." Ironically, most managers seem to get the impression that this means their people want more communication. So they set up two-hour phone conference meetings, and they regurgitate information that was sent in an email and posted on the company's intranet. "More" isn't usually what they are talking about. Their operative words were "communicate well." Creating a plan, a cadence, or a dynamic outline will help you, as a presenter, turn your messages into information that can be consumed by your audience with ease. You've probably never heard this from your team, but if you do these kinds of presentations or calls, I guarantee you, some of them are putting the call on mute and rolling their eyes back in their head. They would never unmute the call and say, "Okay, we've talked about this before, and we received this information in an email yesterday. What is the purpose of this call because if that's all it is, we need to get back to work." Whether on a call, on the web, or in person, a presentation that efficiently communicates specifics, engages their emotions, and leaves them with a feeling of better communication will help you be a better leader. Beyond that, it will increase your brand equity with your team or whomever your audience is.

Being one of the few really great presenters is a skill that will make you stand out in the crowd of highly intelligent and assertive people competing for leadership positions in your world. That's why I call it a "Superpower"—not like Superman or Wonder Woman—but more like Batman or Ironman, just with less money. Once you have proven your value in your trained or professional skills, your ability to present well will add even more value and pay off big time in your career.

Work on One Thing at a Time

I know there may be some of you that will read this book and think to yourself, "Hmm, doesn't everyone know this?" If this is you, think back through the book to the one or two things that stood out to you, and dig into them. Presenting is like anything we do in life, in order to get better at it, you have to practice it. Sure, some people are naturally better at it. I have found in many cases that people who took theater, speech, or debate in high school or college have an innate ability to be more comfortable standing in front of a group. There they learned the basics of projecting, blocking, eye contact, and line delivery. It may have been 30 years ago, but sometimes it's like riding a bike. You just need to get back on and practice it.

For others, this book is overwhelming with all of the techniques and tools to be implemented. If you are just starting out on the presenter's journey, take baby steps. Learn how to overcome your fear of presenting first. Take one thing at a time and perfect it.

I spoke to a professional speaker who told me he felt that even though he was making a great living as a speaker, he believed he could deliver his stories better. He then started studying comedians by documenting how each of them perfected their skill, picking apart how they delivered their stories to get a reaction out of their audiences. Yes, even professional speakers work hard at getting better. Everyone has room for improvement.

Get Better Every Time

Every time you start a new presentation, you should consider it as a reset. Each time, just try to do one thing better. Whatever you do, don't give up if you don't feel that you're getting any better in the short term. This skill takes time and practice.

I was reading a golf book in hopes of improving my game, and I read that one golfer's technique to improve his chipping game was to go to the range in the morning and chip balls on the chipping green. I thought to myself, "Hmm, that would really help." But then I read that he wouldn't leave the chipping range until he had actually dropped one in. He said he would be there for hours, but felt he was actually getting worse. The book then summarized by stating that if you want to improve your game, you need to commit to six hours of practice per day. Whoa! I decided at that point that having a 10 handicap was good enough for me.

Most of you don't aspire to be a professional speaker. You just want to get better at it and improve your value as a professional. Professional speakers work daily on their presentation skills, but you just need to commit to knowing how to present and then practice as much as you can. You will get better because we perfect what we practice. I believe increasing your presentation skills will prove valuable in any business leader's career. It is a differentiating skill in the leadership world today.

So, how do you practice if you don't have many opportunities? Great question, and here is my simple answer: Build presentations on topics about your industry or your passions. Literally go through the entire process of planning and developing them. Develop your cadence, craft your stories, build your slides, and practice them. You may not want to do them in front of a mirror until you're very comfortable with the presentation. By watching yourself, which is a view you will never see when actually presenting, it may throw you off because you will be focusing on how you look versus how you present. Using a mirror once you're comfortable with your content will help you refine your blocking and identify any tics that may be distracting. You can also see body tics by watching your video in fast forward. This may freak you out to see your "presentation dance," but it is revealing if you have habits that you need to work on.

If you are a leader in your company, provide opportunities for your team to develop and present to your group. Help them understand the power of the skill, and give them opportunities to get better. It is a gift they'll thank you for.

Thank you for investing your money and time in this book. I hope you've been able to find a few things that will help you improve. I believe presenting is an understated superpower. I know that if you'll embrace the techniques in this book, you will join the ranks of powerful presenters.

Adding the attribute of a great presenter to your brand will absolutely pay off in your career. The greatest and most influential leaders of our day possess the presentation superpower—now you can as well.

Mike's Top Ten Thoughts

Here are ten things that I feel summarize the experience of this book and will help you get in the right frame of mind.

1. Everyone can get better at presenting.

2. Fear of presenting can be overcome.

3. You'll perfect what you practice.

4. There is no substitution for preparation.

5. Cadence is a critical component in any presentation.

6. Be humble enough to change.

7. Stories connect you to people and their 7-year-old inner child.

8. People want you to be a great presenter.

9. Never give up, just start again.

10. Whatever you do, never put a screen in your presentation that says, "Questions?"

Embracing these thoughts and tactics as you develop your presentation superpower will result in the evolution of a masterful presenter, one that will truly make a difference in the world.

I'll see you out there.

www.ingramcontent.com/pod-product-compliance
Lightning Source LLC
Chambersburg PA
CBHW070803100426
42742CB00012B/2232